# SHEER WILLPOWER

## A Mutiny to Motherhood

Lauri M. Velotta-Rankin

This book is a memoir; however, personal memory is both fallible and biased. To mitigate these limitations, the details stem from meticulously written and referenced notes, emails, and journal entries. To maintain anonymity, names of individuals, organizations, and businesses have been changed.

©2017 Lauri M. Velotta-Rankin. All rights reserved.

All rights reserved. This book or parts thereof may not be reproduced in any form, stored in any retrieval system, or transmitted in any form by any means—electronic, mechanical, photocopy, recording, or otherwise—without prior written permission of the author, except as provided by United States of America copyright law. For permission requests, email lauri@sheerwillpower.com.

Visit the author's website at www.sheerwillpower.com.

Cover illustrated and designed by Lauri M. Velotta-Rankin.

ISBN-13: 978-1545404874
ISBN-10: 1545404879

*Dedicated to*
*Russ & Simone*

LAURI M. VELOTTA-RANKIN

## Crossing the Threshold

*"You do not need to know precisely what is happening, or exactly where it is all going. What you need is to recognize the possibilities and challenges offered by the present moment, and to embrace them with courage, faith and hope."*
—*Thomas Merton*

Stacked to perilous heights, our bags have spent the last two months occupying residency on the living room floor. Their contents, meticulously selected and organized, include shrink-wrapped cases of formula, a portable bassinet, car seat and base, and three large plastic bins filled with an assortment of items a newborn apparently necessitates.

The year is 2012, the sixth of April. My husband, Russ, jests that we should go to bed early in case we receive the call. *The call*—an ambiguous pairing of unimpressive words that happen to represent the most monumental, life-altering event that sets everything in motion. But engrossed in miscellaneous interests, Friday evening escapes us and the lights stay on until sometime after 11PM.

The ring of my cell phone jolts us awake. Just after midnight, my heart races when I see the name illuminated in the dark: Leah. I feel every thud of my rapidly pounding heart and with unsteady hands, I answer,

## SHEER WILLPOWER

"Hi, Leah!" But instead of a female's voice, I'm greeted by Thomas declaring, "She's here!" After an inquiry about both Leah and the baby's health, we inform him that we'll load the car and arrive in five to six hours. When the call ends, Russ and I embrace in a hug teeming with frayed emotion. It has been a very long journey.

We prepare with speed and purpose, intermittently stopping for yelps of joy and exchanged looks of terrified excitement. My cell pings and her face is revealed through a series of photos. We stare and dote. In a penetrating flash, we are overcome with outrageous, vulnerable love.

A few hours into the drive, I ask Russ something we had agreed not to address until we met the baby. We maintained that we wanted to see her face before determining a name, but an acute awareness of the prickly, underlying motive is hidden beneath our words. We simply didn't want to risk it. We refused to bestow a name upon an unborn child who may not remain ours.

But we had already narrowed it to three contenders and with everything proceeding so smoothly over the past few months, I gamble and make a suggestion.

"What do you think about choosing a name?"

We reach New York shortly following a radiant orange sunrise. As the main entrance's sliding doors part, we enter a sensory-rich hospital. The soft hum of hushed voices vibrates alongside ubiquitous chimes and buzzes. Nurses hurry in rubber-soled shoes that whine against glossy vinyl floors. The environment's sterility is supplemented with sudden whiffs of antiseptic.

Although we haven't slept, we're giddy with anticipation. Caffeine is superfluous yet we sip cups of hot coffee to engage our nervous hands. Seated at a small linoleum table in the hospital corridor, the sun's rays illuminate through a succession of windows that climb two stories high. They project spectrums of rainbows across the floor and I convince myself that's a good sign.

Our eyes anxiously search passersby, seeking a reemergence of the social worker. We've derailed her quiet Saturday morning as she decides what to do with us. With no established protocol in place, this hospital was unprepared for our unique circumstance. Further complicating matters, their full-time social worker is home for the weekend and proving difficult to reach. We assist as much as possible, providing a trail of breadcrumbs in the form of names, roles, and phone numbers. We offer the contact information for our agency representative, our Virginia-based social worker, and the local New York adoption lawyer already familiar with our case. We're hopeful she can piece these together and allow us access to the maternity ward. Just past 8AM, visitors are not permitted for five more hours. And without a clear understanding of our role in this baby's birth, that is precisely our identity at this point: visitors.

My cell phone rings and Thomas greets me on the other end of the line. He, Leah, and the baby remain in a postpartum room on a higher floor of the hospital. He tells us that they're excited to finally meet us in person. As he speaks, we hear the high-pitched quiver of a newborn's cry. Electricity surges through my body as the excitement builds. This is the first time I hear her tiny voice.

We learn that our New York-based adoption lawyer is on vacation but in her absence, she sends a social worker, Elizabeth. She will provide copies of all required legal paperwork and coordinate with hospital management and staff.

Upon her introduction, Elizabeth volunteers that she's a mother of two adopted children. She informs us that she will meet with Leah and

Thomas privately to ensure commitment to their plan. Now that the baby has been born, she will ask, outright, if they feel any degree of hesitancy. Elizabeth gently discloses that sometimes, even the most adoption-oriented biological mother reverses course after giving birth. This haphazardly stirs and reawakens the anxiety within me.

Elizabeth suggests we "get comfortable," and we watch as she enters an elevator, vanishing behind its doors. Seated back at our table, we have little to offer distraction. Forced to dull our emotions, we accept the very real possibility that we could find ourselves broken-hearted and driving home in a matter of minutes. Standing at the brink of elation or devastation, we are at the mercy of time.

An hour later, Elizabeth approaches with a relaxed demeanor, a reassuring smile spread across her face. She raves about the young couple's maturity stating that they are unwavering in their choice for adoption. They want the best for this baby and Elizabeth shares that they feel a special connection to us. This sentiment is deeply reciprocated, as Leah and I have developed a relationship with the exchange of weekly emails. My admiration for this young woman, freshly emerged from her teenage years, is massive.

Finally granted access to the maternity ward, we ascend the elevator, escorted by the hospital's social worker. Russ and I are stopped at the restricted area's perimeter while she breaches it with the presentation of a badge. We restlessly watch her exchange with the head nurse, voices inaudible but mouths in rapid motion. Overtly and shamelessly, we stare at them in zealous anticipation, like sprinters crouched at the starting line, ready to bolt forward at the gun's firing.

Their attention is then turned to us and we're motioned forward. Visitor badges are looped around our necks with strict guidance to wear them for the duration of our visit. With a promise to observe this rule, permission is given to meet our daughter, still in the hospital room with Leah and Thomas. We're given their room number and told they're expecting us. And without supervision, we are sent on our way.

Russ and I tightly clutch hands and begin our way down the hospital corridor. I'm certain we're floating because I don't feel my feet strike the ground. Never having experienced so many emotions awakened at once, my entire body is charged and trembling. I retain a pure and unobscured understanding that mere seconds from now will be forever life-changing. As we draw closer, I'm wholly overwhelmed and tears begin to stream down my face.

We cross the threshold into Leah's room.

**SHE**ER **WILL**POWER

LAURI M. VELOTTA-RANKIN

## An Ordinary Life

In my youth, I bemoaned a life too ordinary. I led a cookie-cutter existence, similar to all, unique from none. Simply put, I was a steaming plate of bland chicken.

I imagined a respected family elder recounting her life's tale, surrounded by captivated kin as they absorbed each word with curiosity and wonder. But it never felt as though this would be my future. My legacy was unlikely to slack jaws or raise eyebrows. No gasps of engrossed astonishment would echo from mountaintops.

My childhood best friend was from a bilingual family, enviably rich in culture. Hand-painted works of art from foreign lands were displayed on the walls of her home and intoxicating instrumental music frequently filled the rooms. Adding to this fascinating refinement was the exotic scent of her father's cigar smoke as it infused the air. They frequently traveled to Europe and South America, visiting with relatives and exploring both new and familiar lands. My friend would return home with vivid, exciting stories spilling from her mouth while mixed wood and hammered metal bracelets adorned her arms, the embodiment of an exhilarating adventure abroad.

Meanwhile, my family vacations consisted of sardine-packed cars and long spells of immobility as we traveled north to visit relatives in the suburbs of New York. We'd slide folding chairs and piano benches up to a dining table meant for eight in order to accommodate sixteen. Indulging in extravagant Italian feasts, voices and laughter grew as stomachs swelled with pasta and Chianti seated in straw baskets. At night, beds were quickly occupied, often with two or three kids wedged into a twin. Some slumbered on couches, while others stretched beneath the dining table seeking the additional room.

When reunited with friends, my stories entailed the receipt of matching pajamas gifted to female cousins, no mind paid to age or size. One pair was so large, the crotch hung just north of my knees, causing the spontaneous eruption of an MC Hammer dance for laughs. I'd recount the rebellious coup of cousins draping lit strands of Christmas lights over Grandma while she slept, and the delighted shock when we successfully tricked her into reading the mother of all curse words. My heart now warms with a tremendous sense of appreciation for these treasured moments spent with family. But as an angsty teenager, a phony smile was tacked to my face as I opened a box of pajamas printed with teddy bears and hearts. (Over twenty years later, I not only still possess those oversized teddy bear pajamas, but I wear and cherish them—and occasionally, dust off my personal rendition of "Hammer Time.")

My old journals are placed on the highest shelf of a basement closet, neatly stashed inside a woven basket. Covered in padded white vinyl, my earliest one was a birthday present from a third grade classmate. Personal thoughts and feelings were sloppily scrawled with the assistance of fine-tipped markers in a bevy of colors. Numerous pages were casually littered with my favorite stickers (both puffy and scratch-n-sniff) along with names of friends and their birthdays. A flimsy gold-plated lock protected the secrets of a silly eight-year-old girl who swooned over a boy or ranted about the injustice of a parental restriction.

My second journal assumed a greater level of sophistication with its gilded pages and hardback cover bearing the soft illustration of a teddy bear. Stretched in fluid, formal script across the cover were the words "My Journal," supporting the gravity of my innermost thoughts.

By the fifth grade I grew shrewd, and with the fear of its discovery by a meddling older brother, I hid journal entries within the pages of a spare academic black and white marbled notebook. I even scribbled fake schoolwork into its first few pages hoping this would deter deeper examination. But hidden beyond the "assignments" of fractions and decimals was the content of my most private feelings.

In high school, I utilized our home computer to type and print entries, carefully peeling and discarding the perforated edges. My files were never saved to a hard drive. Instead, I'd erase my words from the screen following each submission.

Shortly after graduating college, I purchased what I retrospectively refer to as my "sad journal," its cover illustration black and moody, well-suited for my sour and glum post-grad persona. Read many years later, its blanketing theme of morbid depression was unsettling, and I considered destroying it. But the recognition that it houses a chapter of my personal history outweighed the desire to torch it. It remains unharmed alongside the other journals, serving as a written archive of my life.

Although the basket's contents matured with age, its overall storyline kept pace with absolute and often deplored normalcy.

But soon this disdained "ordinary life" would veer wildly off-course, twisting and tightening with unabated anguish. I could no longer provide friends updates that weren't met with reactive blends of pity and horror. I became the recipient of a granted wish, but found myself fruitlessly trying to ram the genie back inside his bottle. I yearned for the loving security of the ordinary I had so feverishly railed against.

My keyboard delivered therapy through an outpouring of emotion as I began to document our journey to have a family. And once I felt my feet fully grounded to this earth again, an epiphany arose: rather than confining these stories to four walls of wicker in a basement closet, I recognized the value in shared ownership of this journal. Although the content is specific to my experience, the adversities are collectively ours, denoting life's barriers, hardships, and moments of spirit-breaking. But those are triumphantly trailed by ultimate victory when we refuse to accept defeat's finality.

# Adoption Declaration

When asked about my anticipated future, my childhood ambitions didn't exact an occupation but rather an idol: Barbara Walters. I was addicted to the news program *20/20* and passionately followed their human interest stories. This led to an education about the notorious Romanian orphanages that captured worldwide attention in the early 1990's. Atrocious living conditions exposed rooms littered with bare, filthy mattresses. Soiled and stoic-faced babies listlessly lay in rusted metal cribs that bore more of a resemblance to jail cells than sleeping quarters for children. Cracked paint curled and bubbled on walls, while an evident absence of toys further propagated the heartbreak. The haunting, vacant stares from these children were tragedy personified.

Strangely, tears didn't fill my eyes, but a powerful call to action occupied my heart. Perhaps my youth guarded me from its complexity, the recognition that justice isn't automatically supplied with a set of working lungs. Regardless, this was the precise moment when I felt an acute, fitted purpose. My existence suddenly made sense and enclosed within its chewy center was this decree: I will adopt a child in need. Never before and never since have I felt an objective so purely radiate from my soul. Despite all the directional changes I've taken, all the certainties I inevitably deviated from, this was in perfect

## SHEER WILLPOWER

harmony with my very essence. I proudly affixed the label to my chest: Hello, my name is FATE.

The trail in my wake is permanently etched with innumerable incomplete goals, abandoned when difficulties surfaced and insecurities were exposed. Most that come to the forefront of my mind are career-related feats—*defeats*, to be precise:

1. I once aspired to launch a children's photography business. Enrolling in the applicable classes, I spent endless hours in the darkroom, pouring various chemicals into trays, dodging and burning sections of images to expose the ideal amount of light, and tirelessly reworking images. Eventually, real life trials began and a shocking realization occurred: children don't sit still for the camera, nor do they smile on cue. My ambition fizzled and this goal dissolved.

2. A few years passed and I believed my path to financial success was establishing a video-editing business. Doting parents record endless hours of their children's lives, so I would simply condense the footage into viewable lengths. I painstakingly edited several samples, built a website, designed business cards, and tried selling this concept at a local fair. But in a downward economy, I had few bites. The blemish of another failed venture marred my resume.

3. Unwilling to yield, I found a seemingly simpler undertaking: I would personalize children's clothing with embroidery. So with little experience and too costly a purchase, I splurged on a lavish embroidery machine. I thoroughly read its manual and immediately employed my new knowledge. But as far as failed attempts go, I quickly discovered that this was a time-consuming frustration with miniscule compensation. My interest and its appeal went up in smoke. It was yet another nosedive into the growing pile of bad ideas.

But there was always that one untarnished, pedestal-placed aspiration that wasn't tempered by my failed goals and never affixed with the word "if" but rather "when." And that was adopting a child. Although this childhood mission shared space with the obligations and responsibilities of everyday life, it firmly maintained its place at the table and was never diluted by time's passage.

So in my early 20s, I opened a savings account entitled "Adoption Fund." My chest swelled with pride despite my meager contributions. Like a superhero deflecting harm with mind control or a searing lightning bolt from a fingertip, I had one enormous safeguard on my side: altruism. God, the fates, the universe itself—none would dare derail me from this unselfish endeavor. The facilitating adoption agency and variables related to the child were mere semantics. There were numerous routes to an overabundance of destitute children, and each of my decisions would only lead me closer to my child. I believed there were no wrong turns or untruths in this noble world of adoption because those employed in this humanitarian industry are honorable humans who recognized the final goal as virtuous, just like I did.

But as it turns out, life promises no reciprocal balance and rewards are not delivered the moment you decide to do good.

**SHEER WILLPOWER**

# Kismet

*"You rose into my life like a promised sunrise, brightening my days with the light in your eyes."* –Maya Angelou

Russ and I met at work, a month after he purchased a home and while I was newly under contract for a condo. That, in itself, didn't pose a problem, but their geographical locations certainly did. While my property was in the metropolitan DC-area, his was five hours south in Raleigh, North Carolina. The excitement of a new relationship was offset by a case of unfortunate timing. And as one might suspect, it caused significant frustrations at times. But we were crazy in love and steadfast in our commitment to each other.

Although employed on the same contract, Russ's job was performed remotely, frequently overseas for two to three months at a time. But an unexpected opportunity presented itself in early 2006. Management asked if he was amenable to working on-site for a period of eight weeks. With decent accommodations and daily stipends for meals, Russ accepted with ease. Although neither of us knew it at the time, this pivotal decision helped shape our future relationship.

He had basically just grown comfortable with the placement of office supplies when I began at my new workplace. Since Russ wasn't a regular, on-site employee, my boss struggled to recall his name, clumsily tripping over her words when making our introduction. Russ quickly relieved her, politely extending his hand and stating his name, not a feather ruffled by the blunder. After completing the rounds, I was directed to my office, a mere three doors down from Russ.

Although I had already forgotten the names of the majority of my new coworkers, I remembered his.

If I had a type, Russ was its epitome. He was as handsome as he was kind. He possessed a rare quiet confidence with refreshing humility, despite boast-worthy accomplishments. I was extremely attracted to his positive nature and found the tales of his travels thrilling.

I soon learned that he was an avid runner with a well-disciplined and healthy diet. But a shared Achilles heel, he too lost all resolve at the mere suggestion of sweets. And as it so happened, I kept a desk drawer stocked with an oversized package of Twizzlers. When he'd knock on the metal frame of my opened door declaring his need for "a sugar fix," I'd happily share my stash. It didn't take long before I discovered his passion for Peppermint Patties, so I immediately purchased a bag, despite my relative indifference to the minty discs. It was over these slowly-consumed indulgences that we'd find ourselves chatting longer than newly-acquainted coworkers should.

Eventually, candy wasn't a necessity for conversational breaks. When crossing paths in the hallway, we'd affix ourselves to opposite walls and talk, momentarily stopping to give a polite smile and acknowledge those passing between us. With greater and more obvious office romances blossoming, ours was often overlooked as watercooler fodder.

It was during one of these hallway-courting sessions that I divulged my interest to someday adopt a child. I told him that I was devoutly submitting daily entries for the HGTV Dream Home and that, if successful, I would sell it and use my riches to adopt an army of kids. When I mentioned adoption, Russ's expression revealed pleasant surprise. "That's interesting," he said, "*I* was adopted!"

Our office romance was a whirlwind of excitement but soon brought to an intermission when the eight weeks concluded and he was recruited for a six-week trip to Europe. With unbroken stride, we continued getting to know one another from afar. Lengthy emails and regular texts were soon upgraded to daily phone calls. Shortly after returning home, Russ received his first cell phone bill from that trip, revealing that our long chats cost a whopping $800!

But over time, the novelty of a boyfriend who traveled to foreign lands lost its luster. His deployments became more difficult to endure and I missed him dearly. He would compensate this imbalance by taking time off between trips, and stay with me instead of returning to his home in NC. We spent so much time together, that when deciding to sell his house and move in with me, he counted less than ten nights spent in his Raleigh home. But brick and mortar was simply no match for love.

And so, he changed his zip code.

While our commitment expanded, my condo (intended for one human and her large dog) inexplicably shrunk. Russ set his sights on finding a single-family home. We spent weeks researching communities, visiting model homes, speaking with sales agents, and scrutinizing the details. But Russ expressed lukewarm interest in every house we toured and I resigned myself to the fact that we weren't likely to move anytime soon.

And then while at work one day, I received a call from Russ. He told me about a newly-constructed house located several blocks from my condo and asked if I could meet him there.

The soft yellow house with the oval-shaped window and front porch immediately caught my eye. We walked its empty rooms as the sales agent delivered her pitch, but I didn't absorb her words. Some would argue that the intangible feel of a home is as impressive as its floorplan, and this was no exception. I just *felt* us there.

In February of 2008, Russ and I moved into our new home—along with my beloved Pit Bull, Chase.

I was gifted with the serendipity of meeting Russ. I loved our house, but he was (and remains), home to me. I would have lived in a shoebox with him.

Eight months later, on the bucolic grounds of a French country inn, we married in the exclusive presence of our families. It was simple, yet elegant and perfectly intimate. It was the spectacular birth of our new life together.

## Set Adrift

*"We must let go of the life we have planned, so as to accept the one that is waiting for us." —Joseph Campbell*

I once read that the most appealing tales involve a union of isolation and desperation. But when injected into reality, they're a hostile pairing, equated closer to the violence of a collision than a riveting story. This nasty duo tests the soul's strength and rarely offers clemency. I found myself unwittingly entangled in its web.

Homes neatly arranged on fifth-acre lots in a typical suburban neighborhood quickly negate isolation on the surface. A glance out my back window reveals the details on my neighbor's television screen, and if those adjacent sought a cup of sugar, it could easily be passed through opened windows. But as couples rooted in emotionally-damaged relationships can attest, physical proximity is superficial, and one can sleep inches from a sudden stranger.

By choice, we were living in a community rabid with an exploding population of children. We planned to add to the masses, both biologically and through adoption. But we soon encountered unanticipated complications.

Russ retrieves his mail at our local UPS store while I find two empty window seats at the smoothie shop next door. When he joins me, we sip thick, cold drinks and idly chat as he casually thumbs through the envelopes. His sudden pause of momentum draws my attention to the envelope he rapidly guts. Our first blow arrives on a crisp sheet of linen paper. A medical center's test results were riddled with numeric gibberish, but clearly indicate the impossibility of natural conception. And like a swift, powerful blow to the belly, we feel the air escape our lungs.

An unintentional seclusion is bestowed upon the childless living amongst families. Kindness is largely extended, but it's of a distanced variety, similar to the greeting from a coffee barista. Childlessness had introduced its direct correlation to minimized commonality in the suburbs. When children reside at the epicenter of your existence, it's rational to take less interest in those without. I understood that. I did. But it didn't make life any easier.

We work at building relationships with those living near us, often attending block parties, quarantined between two sets of yellow, child-shaped signs indicating "Caution: Children at Play." I learn about the redistricting of school boundaries, the affliction of childhood eczema, and the difficulty of finding reasonably priced shoes for toddlers. I smile, nod, and stuff my mouth with another bite of potato salad to avoid the expectation of a verbal response. Grateful for the sunshine, my eyes are typically kept hidden behind a pair of dark sunglasses. I struggle to find my role in these conversations. I want to ask about each neighbor's child, excitedly inquire about their personalities and interests, and swoon over their uncanny resemblance to mom or dad. But I can't. My mind is consumed by the challenges of growing our own family. I am an imposter in this environment, a scarlet letter C for "childless" brands the center of my forehead. A pregnant neighbor approaches, and as she pulls close for a hug, I make contact with her distended belly, mere centimeters separating me from the life within her. Emotionally drained, we always find an excuse to leave the party early.

Some couples stumble upon parenthood, dizzy with disbelief, hazily attempting to recall the details leading to this unexpected revelation. Others meticulously plan it, tracking body temperatures and hunting down the hours of peak ovulation. We were never of the former, thought we were grouped with the latter, but eventually found ourselves belonging to an entirely different category. We are unwitting members of faulty biology confronting a vast sea of options with no clear or safe direction.

No map highlights discernable routes, and the reliability of a compass will not be unearthed in a pocket for guidance. This isn't like the sequential evolution of school and no teachers roam these halls pointing the way when lost. Hell, we don't know a single fertility-challenged family, never mind adoptive parents (other than Russ's own). We are essentially left kneading through the emotions and trying to reorient ourselves.

A reengagement of academic skills is now required: rigorous investigation, meticulous analysis, intuitive scrutiny, and a very daunting execution. We are determining the most amenable preferences while exiling the less desirable ones. This learning curve is steep and all-consuming. It is complex, convoluted, overwhelming, and exhaustive.

But just like a new day brings optimism and fresh perspective, I realize that we're at the start of a personal revolution. We're deciding how to bring a child into our family, and there are few things greater. Russ and I are preparing to embark on the most spectacular adventure of our lives, standing at the proverbial road's fork.

However, while the silver lining shimmers, the obscured path unnerves. The range of options is intimidating, limited, and ultimately expensive. We research invasive procedures, learn about orphaned children shackled with exorbitant price tags, and assess the figures in our savings account with unease.

## A Tipped Scale

*"Do not go where the path may lead, go instead where there is no path and leave a trail."* —Ralph Waldo Emerson

Adoption is an easy choice for us, but we have to weigh the pros and cons of domestic versus international. A friend mentions an upcoming adoption fair taking place in the atrium of a nearby mall and emails the specifics. We treat it like we're attending a job fair, dressing the part, arriving early, meeting and greeting each booth's representatives, and fattening our file folder with relevant material. We speak at length with adoption agency personnel as well as adoption lawyers, and our pockets quickly fill with business cards. When we meet a woman employed in the foster care unit of our county government, she informs us of their "foster to adopt" program. Immediately interested, we express our desire to attend the next informational session. We thank her for the insight and bring home the registration form.

I briefly communicate with Beverly, the director of the Foster Care and Adoption Unit, over email. She addresses my questions and once our paperwork is received, delivers the location and time of orientation.

Russ and I arrive at the nondescript, three-story brick building twenty minutes early. We recline our seats and fill the spare time dreaming aloud, the possibilities of our hopes. When we enter the facility, we're directed to a small, narrow room on the second floor devoid of windows. The walls extend no further than three feet beyond the circumference of its conference table. Russ and I are two of the eleven attendees, all eager to learn about the children in our county's foster care system. Everyone politely excuses themselves as they squeeze between the wall and chair backs to find empty seats. Eye contact is scarce and the atmosphere feels oddly tense, as if we're opponents rivaling for a single trophy.

A woman introduces herself and commences with a presentation. We watch a video where a child psychologist describes the emotional trauma often suffered by children who testify in family court. The content is so heartbreaking that I simply cannot look at the screen. My vision is averted, but my ears are exposed, and I hear a child weep as he testifies about a parent's abuse. My husband squeezes my hand under the table. I excuse myself for a bathroom break, unapologetic about missing footage of victimized children. The message has been wholly and clearly received.

When I return to the room, the video is nearing its end with clips of various experts educating about the emotional fragility of foster children. When it ends, the presenter resumes her place at the head of the table. We learn that most children are passed from one foster family to the next as they await the sluggish legal system to determine their fate. It sounds like an outrageously broken system, and judging by her tone, I'm not sure she would disagree with that analysis.

She finally addresses our intention when asking, "Who in attendance is interested in fostering-to-adopt?" Several proud couples raise their hands, ours among them. Dispensing no sugar-coating, she bluntly states that the opportunity is infrequent at best. She tells us about the county's high rate of reunification, hovering around 90%. Their goal is to keep these children with their biological families and she hammers in her point with, "If not mom and dad, mom's parents. If not mom's parents, dad's parents. If not dad's parents, we will search for aunts and uncles." In other words, a cousin twice removed has a better chance to parent than us.

Queue the slamming door.

Though one path dead-ends, we still plan to explore domestic and international adoption. Both options resonate with us. We are already softened to domestic adoption since that was the route taken by Russ's parents. But visiting any one of the many domestic agency websites produces *hundreds* of profiles for waiting couples, many revealing gut-wrenching stories about infertility and miscarriages. I am left with a hollow feeling in the pit of my stomach. Hopeful adoptive parents are essentially vying for the attention and selection of a birth mother (also referred to as a biological mother). While sorting through my thoughts on this, we begin to receive material from international adoption agencies about the scores of children overwhelming orphanages abroad.

Clarity strikes with an intense refocusing of intentions as I am reunited with my childhood declaration. So we make the first major decision in our journey: we will find our child through foreign adoption.

I immerse myself in rigid and systematic research on international adoption. Meticulously combing through the particulars of every accredited agency in the country, the following categories are centered in the red bullseye of my dart's aim:

- ✓ Agencies and their countries/adoption programs*
- ✓ Timeframe, from paperwork submission to returning home with child
- ✓ Ages of available children
- ✓ Political climate and overall stability of country
- ✓ Program strength
- ✓ Visa requirements
- ✓ Number of trips abroad and length of stay required for each
- ✓ Program cost and exclusions
- ✓ Requirements of adoptive parents (ages, years married, etc.)
- ✓ Websites and blogs detailing agency ratings and reviews
- ✓ Better Business Bureau searches on agencies
- ✓ Joint Council on International Children's Services, an advocate and watchdog for orphaned children abroad
- ✓ CIA World Factbook for general information about the country of interest

After months of extensive and often obsessive research, I felt like I was becoming a quasi-authority on international adoption. When asked, as I often was, "What about adopting from [insert name of a country]?" I could definitively declare that they didn't permit adoption from foreign nationals, that their adoption program had been closed for two years, or that the current wait for a child was approximately five years and growing. Some exasperating disqualifiers included exceeding the established age requirements (Russ is nearing forty), misaligned racial identity, and not having enough years of marital bliss under our belts. One program astoundingly required ten years of marriage. Another requested an advanced degree be held by at least one adoptive parent. But the oddest was a condition placed on the adoptive parents' BMI (Body Mass Index). Photos depict soiled chil-

---

* In foreign adoption, the term "program" is synonymous with country name (ie: the program in Ecuador or the Russia program).

dren dressed in threadbare attire, yet somehow, a line is drawn at love handles.

As the layers are peeled and our dissection begins, it is imperative to separate fact from fiction. But sometimes that proves impossible, with no real delineation between the two due to a lack of public information or conflicting reports.

It's unsettling to read about the seedy underbelly of foreign adoption. Some countries had alarming rates of children with fetal alcohol syndrome, a disease undetectable at a young age, but exposed during adolescence when parents often discover its devastating, incurable effects.[†] Other countries were alarmingly linked to deep and widespread corruption, with claims of children kidnapped or outright sold in exchange for food. And then there were the growing concerns about international adoptions programs suddenly terminating without warning. Some adoptive parents, who had waited numerous years and invested large sums of money, were simply left in limbo. Many had already met their children, but they could not bring them home until the country reopened its program, the wait easily spanning several years.

We regularly attend agency seminars and additional adoption fairs. We call, email, and register with over 20 agencies to receive information about their overseas programs. We examine details printed on gloss, satin, and matte paper, some impressively packaged with high-end finishes, while others supply stapled pages printed in black ink, folded and stuffed into a business-sized envelope. We watch DVDs and listen to online podcasts with agency directors venerating their successes alongside gratified adoptive families. Our research drew us stateside as

---

[†] Fetal Alcohol Syndrome is defined as "birth defects that result from a woman's use of alcohol during her pregnancy."
http://www.webmd.com/parenting/baby/features/fetal-alcohol-syndrome

well, investigating programs with birth mothers, state run orphanages, and private orphanages.

We scrub the feet of adoption until they bleed.

# A Promising Start

After extensive research, we finally narrow the field to two adoption agencies. One is headquartered across the country while the other is a mere five hour's drive down the east coast. We reach out to both but immediately reassess our interest in the former. The agency representative was enthusiastic to mail us their DVD, and when it arrived, we were a captive audience. But a contrived sales pitch led with shock value, provoking with images of emaciated and impoverished children back-dropped by deplorable living conditions. An invisible narrator irreverently preached about a responsibility to adopt, while giving very little information about the agency or its actual services. It derailed the viewer from adoption and hurtled them straight into the ditches of child welfare horror stories. Few are ignorant to the plight of orphans, least likely those seeking input about international adoption programs. The mark was clearly missed and we found ourselves more offended than affected by its content.

On the other hand, the relationship I've established with Erica, an employee of the East Coast agency, Murre Adoptions, is fantastic. Our conversations flow with the ease of authenticity, and she awaits a referral through one of the agency's foreign special needs programs.* She is well-informed, quick to reply to my many emails, and I never get the sense that she is trying to sell a product. Erica and I develop a friendship over email and I begin to trust her recommendations and advice.

Russ and I initially express interest in two of their programs, Armenia and Bulgaria. Erica emails a deluge of information, a staggering twenty-six documents for each county. These include the agency's service agreement, adoption procedure, general application, educational requirements, dossier process, and numerous individual PDFs detailing the fee agreement. Despite the astounding volume of material, we are appreciative for this intricate level of detail and judiciously read through every page.

We reach a decision and move forward with the Armenia program with Murre. When I learn that my mom has a business trip in the same town as Murre's home office, we plan a road trip together. I email the agency and inquire about an in-person meeting with the director, Lilith Winston. Russ leaves town for work but my mom will serve as a second set of ears. Prior to his departure, Russ and I compose a list of questions for this engagement. With packed bags and a hopeful heart, we head south.

The morning of my meeting with Lilith, I'm filled with the anxiety of a prospective new hire. Dressed in professional attire, I take another glance in the full-length mirror before leaving the hotel room. It's not a job interview—and my role is actually more analogous to a hiring manager—but I still strive to make a good impression on Lilith.

---

\* Synonymous with "match," the term "referral" signifies the identification of a child (made by the in-country partners) for the prospective adoptive parents. http://adoption.about.com/od/adopting/bb/strtadoptproces.htm

## SHEER WILLPOWER

The adoption agency is situated in the corner of a commercial building's first floor. A handful of opened office doors are nestled around a receptionist's desk. With heightened senses, I try to absorb the intangibles of the atmosphere, hoping it will whisper in the ear of my intuition. I so badly want this agency to be the right fit, and I am as nervous as I am excited.

My mom and I are greeted warmly and escorted into Lilith's empty office. We sit in the two chairs closely positioned opposite her desk. I remove my laptop from its bag opening the file with our questions. I am ready.

A few moments later, Lilith arrives. Her kind eyes and warm charm melt my anxieties. Lilith divulges that she's the mother of two adopted children. She not only manages the agency, she's been through the adoption process firsthand. I already feel like this is a destined match.

When asked which program we'd like to pursue, I firmly and proudly state "Armenia." I promptly begin tapping on my laptop's keyboard as she articulates the history of Murre's success in Armenia. She breezes past the program's expense but it's such a shock, I hear nothing following the stated figure. Lilith recommended families have access to $25,000 *more* than the amount quoted in the material Erica had supplied.† I felt sucker-punched but my skepticism radar fails to launch.

Deflated, I admit to Lilith that this is simply out of our range. With our latest fertility challenges at the forefront of my mind, we can't allocate this significant portion of a budget towards a single adoption. Lilith pauses, furrowing her eyebrows in problem-solving mode. She

---

† I later inquire about the considerable difference via email and Lilith directs me to a page buried within those twenty-six documents, an ambiguous: "additional expenses to be considered."

abruptly springs forward in her chair planting her hands, palms down, on the desk, like she's instantaneously been imparted with divine knowledge. Murre is preparing to launch in a new program in Morocco and she enthusiastically shares a scattering of facts. Having recently returned from visiting the partnered orphanage in a small town called Meknes, Lilith praises its condition, declaring it the best of all her programs. Apparently extremely uncommon, she saw thirty to forty infants and excitedly gushes about the phenomenal and rare advantages this program will offer. My notes include:

- ✓ The facility's director is very accommodating to foreigners
- ✓ The wait for a referral is short compared to most adoption programs
- ✓ There is a two-trip requirement, totaling less than three weeks: one visit to meet the children and another to bring them home
- ✓ The children receive medical examinations by an American-trained doctor
- ✓ Gender preferences are allowed
- ✓ The adoption of multiple children is permitted, whether siblings or unrelated
- ✓ The cost is still being determined, but she is confident it will fall within our range

Additionally, she reveals that although unofficial, they currently have only two families awaiting registration. So if we move quickly, we could find ourselves third in line—and in the world of foreign adoption, that is astounding. Russ and I will have to expedite our paperwork because as Lilith forewarns, this will be a very popular program and its waitlist will grow quickly.

The stars have aligned. I believe she is entrusting us with a great secret and I'm oozing with gratitude for being its recipient. I express serious interest in this incredible opportunity, but reiterate that cost is really a key factor.

A few days later, I receive an email from Lilith asserting, "As for the Moroccan fees – we really hope this program will be less than 20K all said and done." This cost is so shockingly low, that we express interest in adopting two babies.

My Mom had sat beside me for the duration of this meeting with Lilith. In the beginning, she was alive with questions, but she grew silent by its close. She didn't expose any physical or verbal indications of apprehension, but I wondered what was brewing behind those probing eyes. On the car ride back to the hotel, she delicately expressed her reservation. She sensed that Lilith was "too much of a salesman" and reminded me of the old adage, "If it sounds too good to be true…" Not only did I disagree, I didn't want to even consider the possibility that she could be right.

But her instinct was spot-on, while mine malfunctioned with ear-piercing explosions and sparks bright enough to light the night's sky.

# "Aunt" Catherine

Our first cashier's check is delivered to Murre, the one laden with a throat-constricting abundance of zeros, and the stopwatch ignites with rapidly climbing numbers.

Lilith informs us that a "home study" is our top priority. We soon learn that this easy-going term is actually a mental pap smear. A home study bequeaths a social worker access to the personal aspects of your marriage, families, friendships, finances, and overall lifestyle with analytical precision. And it's a multi-directional review, looking to your past, present, and future. A legal requirement for all avenues of adoption, the home study is an imperative evaluation for safeguarding the life of an adopted child. However noble, it awkwardly and uncomfortably exposes privacies to a stranger: the case social worker.

The specifics differ state-to-state, but ours requires three in-person visits conducted over a period of several months. Although Murre conducts these for their in-state residents, they aren't licensed in Virginia, so they send us a list of local agencies to consult.

Also a resident of Virginia, Erica recommends the agency she used, The Lillian Foundation. Our case is assigned to its co-founder, Catherine Hardy, and Erica is elated by this match. She reassures me that

Catherine executed her home study with efficiency and speed. "You'll be pleased," she confidently declares.

The first of our visits is scheduled at The Lillian Foundation's home office. Per our habit, Russ and I arrive considerably early and remain in the car to review our notes one last time. We are armed with a binder filled with paperwork Murre provided, copies of our birth certificates, and freshly dusted off for this venture, our checkbook. Its presence is gaining in popularity. We vacate our car ten minutes prior to our scheduled appointment and head inside.

The interior is unexpected and odd, assuming more of a resemblance to a townhome than an office. We're led up a narrow staircase that releases tired creaks with each step. At the top, a hallway exposes four doors and I'm convinced we're about to walk into the bedroom of someone's home.

Escorted into one of the rooms, Catherine coolly introduces herself from behind a desk. Likely in her mid-sixties with dark, weary eyes, Catherine is polite, but solemn in manner. I don't envision her being easily brought to laughter.

She slides a lengthy checklist across her desk towards us and begins explaining the items and our responsibility to obtain each. These are necessary for the completion of our home study. The list includes individual medical reports from our physicians, notarized financial statements, fingerprints taken by our local police department, child abuse clearances from the FBI (and similar forms from the Department of Homeland Security), three personal letters of recommendation, coursework related to parenting internationally adopted children, and so on.

She dryly informs us that the speed of our pursuit is in direct correlation to the home study's completion. With animated enthusiasm, I tell her about Murre's short wait for Morocco and assure her of our desire to move swiftly. She is unaffected by our motivation, and I suspect that she's heard similar declarations made many times before.

Catherine stands to signal our meeting's conclusion and following suit, we rise. She leads us down the staircase to the receptionist's desk and before parting, I extend my hand for a shake and express appreciation for her service. For the first time, her ruby-painted lips part for a smile, exposing exceptionally white teeth beneath.

With a growing desensitization to these large figures, another check is carefully torn from its residence to cover the price of our home study. And like assessing the cost of extra toppings on a pizza, a list of additional fees are explained, including edits to the final home study, individual notarizations, and photocopies.

Our second home study is scheduled at our house four weeks later. Knowing that Catherine will request a walk-through, we spend hours scrubbing everything from toilets to baseboards, even organizing the interiors of closets. We prepare coffee and neatly arrange our completed forms on the kitchen table.

Privately, Russ and I refer to her "Aunt" Catherine to ease the invasiveness of her questions and embrace her quirky nature. But our biggest concern is less about the questions she'll ask and more about her reaction to meeting Chase—large, loveable, and extraordinarily hyper when meeting new people. Striking us as somewhat rigid, we don't anticipate Catherine enjoying 90-pounds of happiness encircling her in a moat of drool. So instead of permitting his usual freedom to roam the house, we confine him to the basement for the duration of her visit. He defiantly plants himself against the door that separates us and protests with dramatic, chirping whines. Upon Catherine's arrival, she pauses at our home's entrance and asks if we own a bird.

## SHEER WILLPOWER

We extend the invitation of introducing her to Chase, but not surprisingly, Catherine declines—and we breathe a sigh of relief.

In less than two months, we receive our completed home study from Catherine, and we are thrilled with the quick turnaround time. But as we begin to read through the seven-page document, our excitement twists to unexpected disappointment. It is riddled with careless errors, like the repeated misspelling of my first name. Russ's employment is incorrect and references to our individual medical reports are misdated, for us both. There is mention of daycare despite asserting my plans to stay home and the name of a personal reference is misspelled. Additionally, we had clearly stated our intention to adopt two children at once, but the document consistently addresses a single child. And the biggest zinger was a statement about our desire to add biological children to our family, when we imparted Catherine with the very personal details of being "reproductively-challenged."

We note a total of *twenty* mistakes within those seven pages, which seems inexcusable. There's a hard-to-deny irony regarding the deep scrutiny executed on our lives, yet the sloppiness of its collective review as an official document.

It takes Catherine a perplexing, head-scratching three weeks but the corrections are made and our home study is finalized. We submit it to Murre.

LAURI M. VELOTTA-RANKIN

# Take It or Leave It

*"Take the first step in faith. You don't have to see the whole staircase, just take the first step." —Dr. Martin Luther King, Jr.*

The abundance of paperwork required for international adoption is quite extensive yet amusingly contradictory with its dainty, French-derived name, dossier ('däsē). Amassing the material is a monumental task that takes us over four months to complete. We roam electronic halls and wait in physical lines at various local and federal government offices spread across the DC-area. Gathering piles of documentation, hours are spent hunched over the kitchen table as we work to decipher a migraine-inducing series of codes and cryptic questions. Tedious, bureaucratic forms are slowly crossed off our list. A required thirty-five credits include a class in CPR, reading pre-approved books on adoption, and meeting with a Moroccan family. Online courses in foreign adoption include passing tests for advancement. Collectively, our dossier is twenty-eight pages thick.

Adoption agencies often advise their international program families that dossiers typically take four to six months to assemble. When inquiring about the wait for a child in a particular country, this chunk of time is not included. And when registering with an agency, your information is not passed along to the foreign country or orphanage

## SHEER WILLPOWER

until the dossier has been provided in its entirety. In other words, it is not only essential to the adoption process, but it is the ticket stub permitting you to stand in an imaginary line outside the orphanage's front door.

We've currently invested nine months in this program, five of which have been spent standing in this theoretical line—but it is peanuts compared to many popular programs that entail a two to five year wait.

Not for the financially faint of heart, but it's worth addressing international adoption costs. Our expenses include an international fee of $4,500, a wiring fee of $800, and a $2,000 mandatory donation fee. Yes, this is actually itemized as a "mandatory donation," with the bold-face and underlined word "non-optional" placed besides the oxymoron. The explanation for the international fee is a breakdown of obscurely-stated services such as "additional paperwork" and "contingencies." In more boldface font, the agency appends that these "are considered reasonable and customary," so we oblige, proceeding with blind trust.

It's become routine in this process to write checks, and we barely flinch as new costs surface. So we aren't too surprised when, eight months after signing with our agency, we receive an email containing an addendum of fees. But it delivers a bombshell with costs that double the international fee and orphanage donation, totaling just shy of nine thousand dollars. We know unexpected costs will arise but never ones that bump the initial overall cost nearly 50%. As mentioned earlier, it was just a few short months ago when Lilith wrote, "As for the Moroccan fees – we really hope this program will be less than 20K all said and done."

We pay the additional fees and don't hear from our agency unless we send a message asking about updates. They tell us that the next time we hear from them should be to congratulate us on a referral.

Then late one weekday evening, everything changes when we receive an email from Lilith. The subject line declares, "Call me around 930a please." The body of her message only comprises the number to her direct line. We are convinced this will be *the call*.

We arrive at work the following morning around 7:30AM, and I can't fathom how I'm supposed to retain composure for the next two hours. Is this the call informing us that we have an active referral? Have they found our children? I don't think I've ever felt such intense anticipation.

I have the focus of a toddler and hope no one approaches me seeking intellectual conversation. I am distracted, a million miles away, and just spilled my morning cup of coffee in my employer's kitchen. In a virtual trance, I watch as it spreads and cascades over the counter's edge and down the cabinet doors, producing an expanding brown puddle on the floor. I clean it with automated motion and no sense of urgency.

In two short hours, our lives may be forever altered. Currently, these children are nothing more permanent than a deep-seated desire. We could finally be connected with them, even if only by words. I am overwhelmed with this very likely possibility, as the agency director doesn't typically reach out to waiting clients for lesser reasons.

I visit the deli downstairs from my office, purchasing a cup of fruit and banana walnut muffin. And with my newly-prepared cup of coffee, I eat breakfast at my desk and try to give my workload some semblance of attention. But what repeatedly steals my concentration is the knowledge that today I may learn about my children. *My children.* I realize it's just a connection through words, but an emotional charge is carried through their current.

Opting to make this call with greater privacy than a closed office door could provide, Russ and I decide on the confines of our parked car. I am fearful of disappointment but vibrating with excitement. We are already familiar with the level of detail furnished in a standard first call for adoptive parents once a referral has been established. Information is provided about the child's gender, age, medical history, and a photo is commonly delivered as well. I wonder what else we may learn. Perhaps their emailed pictures will be awaiting us once we return to our offices. I imagine what it will be like to finally see their faces, never to be forgotten.

But our call doesn't proceed as expected.

Lilith's greeting is upbeat and our confidence swells that good news awaits. She begins by offering her congratulations. Murre's Moroccan partners have identified a baby girl for us and request that we travel to Morocco the following week. She adds the caveat that the baby has "an unknown medical condition" and unfortunately, the American-certified doctor is unavailable to visit her for a diagnosis. Lilith also informs us that the baby is not from the orphanage she had raved about in Meknes. Instead, we'll be traveling to an orphanage in the capital city of Rabat. There is no mention of the second child, so Lilith assures us that she will inquire. She reminds us that baby boys are readily available in Morocco, so we shouldn't be concerned.

No further information is provided. We're given no details about the baby's age, no photos have been mailed or emailed, and her medical condition is a complete mystery. This is a highly unusual circumstance for international adoption, and Lilith recognizes that. We ask if she can try to acquire additional information before we travel, but she bristles, delivering an ultimatum: if we are not comfortable moving forward with the details she has already offered, she will move to the next family in line. She then asks what we'd like to do. Russ and I look at one another, nerves ablaze with concern, but excitement and optimism prevail.

And again, we proceed with blind trust.

**SHEER WILLPOWER**

# New Life of a Different Kind

Our home was erected on a razed lot of flat land. Once completed, the builder planted a small Crape Myrtle tree in each yard, neatly positioned between the house and sidewalk. Ours blooms white while most around us flourish in shades of pink or violet. Maybe it was an accidental mislabeling, but I happen to love its white flowers that resemble tiny sheets of crumpled paper. It continues to grow heartily and healthily, competing with none for sunshine and rain water, as it maintains its reign as the only tree on our entire property.

While the front yard was neatly landscaped with a variety of green shrubs, the backyard was a barren rectangle struggling to sustain grass. We aspire to develop this outdoor space with a deck, trees, flowers, and a vegetable garden. We could hang a feeder from a tree and include a pedestaled bird bath in a plot landscaped with flowers. I envision the soft glow of string lights draped above a dining table as Russ plays his guitar and I indulge in a slice of chocolate cake as the sky darkens.

These dream-clouds vanish as reality impolitely elbows its way in. After bills are paid, our bank account surplus is funneled directly to adoption expenses. Financial prudence is the villain that has kept our yard unembellished. It has simply become a luxury, while growing our family is our personal necessity.

A few days before leaving for Morocco, Russ visits a local nursery. "A single tree," he suggests. "I'd like to get a Maple tree for our backyard." A minimal expense, I think it's a great idea. Russ scours the selection of trees, meticulously analyzing leaves, trunks, and roots for signs of good health. He eventually settles on a young, healthy maple and makes the purchase.

The nursery's availability for delivery and installation is while we we're overseas in Morocco. I fall in love with the timing and its symbolic representation of adding life to our home. One day, we could tell our children that while we were working on their adoption in their native land, this tree was finding new life in our yard. It felt like a spiritual parallel between our children and this tree.

And so, with a small orange flag supplied by the nursery, Russ and I survey our property to find the best location for our new tree's home. We agree upon a site and Russ plunges the flag's stake into the earth.

## A Golden Olive Branch

*"Sometimes you will never know the value of a moment, until it becomes a memory." –Dr. Seuss*

The particulars concerning accommodations typically serve as a backdrop, generally offering an interesting visual for a reader, yet it's somewhat inconsequential to the overall story. Ours, however, was pivotal. It not only held considerable relevance but it was an unconventional arrangement gifting a profound and invaluable relationship.

Good friends and neighbors, Adam and Kirsten, were familiar with our adoption and sudden call to travel. Born in Morocco, Adam's relatives are spread throughout the country but largely concentrated in Rabat. While we journey to northern Africa, his mother was planning the reverse route to spend a month with his family in the states. With her encouragement, he graciously invited us to spend our two weeks abroad at her home in the city. Unable to refuse such generosity, we had accepted.

The following day, Adam called with an update. His mother, Haja, deferred her travel by a week and now anticipated hosting us. Our proposal to stay at a hotel for those seven days was outright rejected.

We were apprehensive to burden her with our visit, but he convinced us that she'd love the company. So we agreed with tremendous gratitude… and a bit of trepidation.

A second call arrived from Adam two days prior to our departure. He informed us that Haja had opted to delay travel for a full month and despite having never met us, she kindly insisted on accommodating our entire stay in Rabat.

Admittedly, we began to worry, wondering what we had gotten ourselves into. Being a houseguest to someone you never met is quite the imposition in itself and rather awkward for all parties involved. But we also do not share a common language, religion, or culture with Haja. She is a devout, Arabic-speaking Muslim woman in her sixties who has spent her entire life in Rabat. We also discovered that there is no feasible way for us to communicate with her. Referencing a translation book would not help as she is unable to read. Russ purchased an audible translation tool but it proved ineffective when Adam tested it. We learned that local family members speak fluent English and will assist us with regular visits. With our disruption extending beyond Haja, we hesitated. But Adam reaffirmed that everything will be fine. A hotel room for those weeks in Morocco would exceed $1,000, and with the barrage of increasing costs, we accepted their extraordinarily kind offer of hospitality.

Our adoption is essentially a leap of faith. What's one more jump?

As a contingency, we scribbled down the name and phone numbers of several nearby hotels and packed it along with our belongings. But we never referenced it.

Our course of travel is from Washington, DC to Paris, and then Paris to Casablanca. Twelve hours after leaving our home, we finally arrive

## SHEER WILLPOWER

in Morocco. We're bursting with joy while tempering a restless fear of possible disappointment. The one emotion that rises to the top is our utter astonishment at this tangible progress and the fact that we're inhaling our first breath of Moroccan air.

Lilith had supplied the name of Murre's counterpart facilitator, Nada, who we've been instructed to meet at the airport coffee shop. She will escort us to our host's home in Rabat and outline the itinerary for our two-week stay. But we have no further information on Nada. No physical description was offered and we don't even know her last name. When Russ asked Lilith if we could have Nada's phone number, a reasonable measure of security, she cited a legality that prohibited it. So we wait to be approached.

A grinning young woman draws near, stating our names with confidence like we're already well-acquainted. Realizing this must be Nada, we practically spring from our chairs with relief and introduce ourselves.

I hadn't given much thought to the identity of our in-country contact. Perhaps I just assumed we'd be meeting a female not unlike the many professionals I encounter daily, outfitted in a sharp pant suit and speaking with composed focus. Or some variation of this woman. But Nada boldly breaks the hinges off this box I had constructed. Her bubbly personality compliments the smile that rarely deserts her mouth. Her fashion sense is on-trend with the latest seen in stylish magazines, pairing tight, dark jeans with a cropped brown leather jacket. We're surpassed by her modernity, as she carries a cell phone more current and "blingy" than either of ours. Although Muslim, she opts not to cover her head with a hijab. But what I notice above all else is her very youthful appearance. I wouldn't have flinched if she told me she was sixteen years old.

Nada helps with our luggage and guides us to a sedan idling curbside. She tells us that her friend is our driver, and while the young man politely greets us, he remains silent for the trip's duration. I don't know if that's intentional or due to a language barrier. Nada bounces into the passenger seat while we climb in back. As we begin the hour-long drive to Rabat, she twists her body to face us and we engage in conversation. Her comfort-level with us seems instant and it's quickly reciprocated. Nada is delighted to hear that we live near Washington, DC, expressing her desire to visit. "Soon," she declares. She talks about her family and discloses her age: twenty-three years old. In this seemingly complex field of work, I can't help but wonder about her experience.

Within twenty minutes of meeting her, Nada excitedly talks about a teaching position she's considering in the US. She also manages to reveal that she is Murre's sole Moroccan employee. I try to keep my expression neutral and tighten my jaw, denying its bottom to drop. This in-country partnership has a single point of failure, despite Murre's reference to their "in-country partners." And she is prattling on about this thrilling new job opportunity. Nada has unintentionally exposed some troubling information during this car ride. And we haven't even arrived in Rabat.

Finding no appropriate way to ask what would happen should she resign, we focus on the identified child. We excitedly ask for details about the baby girl selected for us, but Nada offers the equivalence of a verbal shrug with no insight to share. In fact, she has never met or seen a picture of the baby. But she says that we'll visit the orphanage the next day and exhilaration immediately replaces disillusionment. If we're going to the orphanage where this child resides, it stands to reason that we'll meet her.

## SHEER WILLPOWER

Nada is elated that we'll be staying with a Moroccan, and kindly proposes to help with translation. She'll spend as much time with us that day as we'd like, and we are grateful for Nada.

The sparse landscape begins to grow dense with buildings and pedestrians, and we're soon weaving through the busy city of Rabat. Though Morocco is known for their olive trees, we're surprised to find the streets lined with orange trees. Their brightly-hued orbs dot the foliage with a sweet fragrance that scents the air.

The car settles into a parking space along the street outside Haja's home and we vacate along with Nada. Haja lives in a central location within the city, adjacent to an art gallery and a few short blocks from Rabat's Grand Mosque. This neighborhood appears newly renovated and modern.

We ring the bell and Haja opens the door to her floor-level condo, welcoming us in with the familiar smile reflected on her son's face. She stands just shy of five feet and has rich, brown eyes and olive skin, similar to my Italian complexion. Haja is modestly clothed in a multicolored tunic and a silk scarf faintly exposes a gray hairline. She is a widow, mother to nine adult children and numerous grandchildren. While maintaining a very gentle nature, Haja projects dignity and strength. It's really quite inexplicable but I've never felt a presence like hers. Haja radiates a spiritual serenity.

She and Nada exchange warm greetings, "As salaam alaikum!" These beautiful words translate into English as "Peace be onto you." I grow very fond of this tender salutation bestowed upon us by strangers throughout our travel in Morocco. It is as commonplace as "Hello" in the US.

Haja beckons us into her home and my eyes dance around the room. A variety of woven rugs in muted palettes cover the creamy marble floors. The white walls are adorned with family photos and artwork, extending to tall ceilings and intricate molding. A dining and living room share a large space just past the home's entrance. Haja walks us to an enclosed room lined by deep couches along its walls, neatly arranged with embellished pillows. An opened window at the far end of the room reveals the conversation of chattering birds. Although there's an inelegance to our inability to communicate, an enigmatic peace settles into my bones.

An older gentleman seated on the couch rises to his feet and Nada explains that he is Haja's brother, here to welcome us. The phone then rings and after a few spoken words, Haja hands me the receiver. I converse with her daughter, Nadia, who lives in Casablanca. She speaks fluent English and inquires about our flight, asking if we are comfortable and if she can help answer any questions. I gush with appreciation that I hope she can relay to Haja and we then say our goodbyes.

Haja sets a metal serving tray on the table before us, displaying sweets and Moroccan mint tea in hand-painted glasses. Although not an avid tea drinker, this tastes like heaven and we happily receive it multiple times a day. We never tire of drinking Haja's fabulous mint tea or her rich black coffee.

Russ and I fall silent while Nada and Haja engage in animated conversation. Despite not understanding their words, I can see that Nada is very respectful of Haja, and if first impressions speak truths, they seem to genuinely like one another.

Nada tells us that we'll be sleeping in the condo's only bedroom which is Haja's. We immediately oppose and emphatically decline, but recognizing our head nods, Haja laughs and waves her hands in our direction like she's slowly swatting at a fly. Nada smiles and informs, "She insists." We don't know how to protest it any further without offending and find ourselves tongue-tied.

We ask some basic questions about Haja's home, habits, and schedule, and having learned "thank you" in Arabic, we offer a very heartfelt "Shukran, Haja. Shukran."

Whenever I speak these words to Haja, my hands instinctively draw to my heart.

When Nada leaves that first day, we email Lilith the update she had requested. We detail our arrival, Nada's assistance, and the loveliness of our host. She replies with a message from Nada, noting her charges for the day. Perplexed and unaware of any daily charges, we inquire. Lilith responds, "Oh Laurie, I am searching my emails to you for travel and I can see that I sent a set out to everyone — but you and Russ. I am so embarrassed and upset." She then explains that Nada charges sixty dollars per five hours of her time, whether escorting us to the courthouse to file paperwork or joining us for lunch. Factoring this fee into our two week stay could easily exceed a thousand dollars.

The oversight annoys me because it isn't the first time information has failed to reach us. It also places additional stress on our finances. But recognizing that there are so many moving parts to this process, I adapt to inevitable missteps. Besides, we have a more pressing matter to address with Lilith. This baby girl has a medical complication and we had asked for an update on the doctor's diagnosis. Her reply is bafflingly brief. "There is not a US board certified doctor in Rabat, nor will the orphanage permit any doctor to visit the child/ren."

LAURI M. VELOTTA-RANKIN

# Dismantled Emotions

The following morning, we pack an accordion folder stocked with seven copies of our dossier and walk to the Rabat train station to meet Nada. From there, we'll catch a cab to the orphanage. The magnitude of this occasion is profound, and our feet strike the pavement with speed and focused purpose. Overcome by nervous anticipation, I remind myself to remain calm and breathe. We pass the art museum, navigate through and across busy city streets, and arrive a mere ten minutes after leaving Haja's home. The station is bustling and we wonder how we'll find Nada in the crowd. But we soon spot her and wave our arms above our heads to catch her attention. She greets us kindly and asks about our evening with Haja. We then load into a cab she hails and the butterflies awaken in my belly. I suspect the events of this particular day will forever be ingrained in my memory.

The taxi veers off the main road and settles in front of a set of iron gates. A uniformed security guard cautiously observes us as we empty out of the cab. Nada greets him from the street and after a brief exchange, he unlocks the gate to permit our entrance. We swap passports for visitor badges. His manner is curiously terse as he directs us to ensure the badges remain outside our jackets for visibility. We oblige, and presumably satisfied, he turns his back to us, returning to his station.

The orphanage is comprised of several buildings, resembling a small college campus. As we walk towards the main building, three school-aged boys watch at us, standing motionlessly in the grass. Each child appears to possess some degree of intellectual disability, and one is confined to a wheelchair. We smile and wave hello but they just stare back, attentive but indifferent to our presence. We do not see, nor hear, any other children—which is surprising, considering the orphanage's size.

Ushered to a bench in a sparse hallway, we sit while Nada meets with the director behind closed doors. We assume we'll be called to join them shortly. Ten minutes pass, followed by fifteen more. Half an hour later, the director's door swings open and Nada motions us inside. What we hadn't known at the time was that this wasn't just our first meeting with the director, but it was Nada's as well.

Rania serves as the director of the Rabat orphanage. She is an attractive woman whose uncovered hair is conservatively drawn back into a tight bun. Fluent in French and Arabic, she does not speak English, so Nada's translation is necessary. Rania greets us with compulsory politeness but there's an unmistakable lack of warmth, and a palpable tension hangs in the air as she rarely makes eye contact with either Russ or me. We are respectful and quiet, trying hard to meet the expectations of our host. But despite our best efforts, Rania's demeanor is hard to misconstrue. She simply appears to dislike us.

While she takes a phone call, Nada informs us that Rania recently developed an acute distrust of Americans. She details the story of an American journalist who posed as a volunteer to expose the living conditions of this orphanage shortly before our arrival. We later research the incident, but find no such exposé.

After learning of this ill-timed news, it is no surprise when Rania coolly declines our offer to volunteer in the orphanage while in

Morocco. Nada suggests a change of heart once we acquire the local judge's approval scheduled later that week, but all we can do is nod in compliance and hope she's right.

A barrage of fast-talking conversation ensues and Nada pauses to interpret. Her expression reveals discomfort and I sense bad news awaits. There are no children available for adoption here, and they have a substantial waitlist. But that was not all. We are stunned to learn that our dossier, the one we had worked so hard to expedite months ago, had never been submitted, placing us behind every other waiting family.

When adopting internationally, calls to travel typically indicate that your dossier has reached the front of the line. So why are we here? Still, we smile politely, careful not to offend with our confusion and disappointment.

Rania and Nada resume their conversation in Arabic, with no inclusion or translation. Moments later, a caretaker ushers a little girl named Sarah into the room. Something is whispered in Sarah's ear and she gingerly walks towards me. She is smiling, bearing the sweet, familiar face of a child with Down syndrome. I'm thrilled to meet her and gently reach out my hands, a gesture to see if she'd like to sit in my lap. She agrees and I pull her onto me, happy for the contact with a child. Sarah shows immediate affection, stroking my hair and repeatedly kissing my cheeks. She hands her doll to Russ and he makes it dance, sending Sarah into a fit of adorable giggles. Nada tells us that Sarah is four years old. The room falls silent and I feel their analysis. I wonder if they're assessing us, perhaps noting our treatment of a child with special needs. But then Sarah moves in closer to me, her face mere inches from mine, and she speaks just one, heart-shattering word.

"Mama."

## SHEER WILLPOWER

We had been summoned to Morocco because of an adoptable baby girl. Is Sarah the reason we are here?

I snap a stunned look at Russ, then immediately at Nada, my countenance begging for an explanation or clarification. Nada softly states that Sarah is available for adoption. It's a wicked entanglement and I'm horrified because at this very moment, they are awaiting our answer. My throat constricts and I'm panicked, uncertain I can keep tears from escaping my eyes. Before I can even find my voice, Nada pacifies telling us that should we "pass," another family with Murre is a good match. They had just wanted to give us the option.

The nurse calls Sarah back to her, and hand-in-hand, they leave the room.

I've hardly had time to process what just transpired. Emotionally dismantled, I feel a deep sense of betrayal, and search my husband's face for guidance. His jaw is clenched and he bears an expression of tongue-bitten resentment. Russ and I are given no opportunity to speak privately.

An orphan was instructed to show me affection and call me "Mama" while they asked if we wanted her, right in front of this child. Russ and I are subjected to this unethical and despicable ploy, but my heart aches for its cruelty to Sarah. How will they explain that the woman they suggested she refer to as her mother is, in fact, *not*? And how often do they pull this unscrupulous scheme on unsuspecting, hopeful couples?

These thoughts whirl through my mind like a blinding and disorienting sandstorm while we sit in Rania's office. The most bizarre part of this episode is that while we're both reeling from what just occurred, the women around us react with indifference, as if we had declined their offer for a cup of tea.

Despite it all, our hearts are so deeply attached to this Moroccan adoption and we still yearn for its success. Ever-hopeful, we have Nada ask Rania if we can purchase supplies for the children. Rania eagerly grabs her pen and begins scribbling down a list.

She also asks if we can buy her lunch.

Outside the orphanage, we catch a cab with Nada to Morocco's superstore, Marjane. Marjane is a monstrosity of a warehouse, a supercenter with aisles of groceries adjacent to racks of clothing and electronics. Rania's list is comprised of modest essentials like soap, diapers, toilet paper, and butter. After gathering each item, Russ and I add bags of cookies, dried fruit, and nuts. We grab replacements for the food we've consumed at Haja's, including treats for her as well. Nada makes the selection for Rania's lunch, and we head back to the orphanage in a taxi, its trunk filled with the goods.

We still do not see, or even hear, any children.

**SHEER WILLPOWER**

# Taking Shelter

*"The light at the end of the tunnel is just the light of an oncoming train."*
—Robert Lowell

Upon our return from the orphanage, we're greeted at the door by Haja and her three adult daughters. Nada is with us, and they eagerly pepper her with questions.

You become well-attuned to body language when you don't understand the verbal one, and what I witness in their reactions worries me. I can see the flashes of confusion on their faces as they listen to Nada speak in their shared tongue. In particular, the expression of one daughter is most altered. Her smile vanishes and eyes narrow, fixed on Nada. I believe she's conveying what I fear most: suspicion.

Being summoned overseas and not meeting the child explicitly identified for us was concerning. But we thought that perhaps this is a common practice for Moroccan adoptions, or specific to this individual orphanage. However, Nada clearly appears uneasy as she composes her answers to their many inquiries.

When the daughters' complete their interrogation on our behalf, Nada departs and the mood lightens. The evening brings two new introductions, Nabil and Yasmin.

Nabil is Haja's fifteen-year-old grandson. Speaking fluent English, he is a friendly, precocious, and reverent young man. We chat about his schoolwork and future plans, and I marvel at the maturity I certainly didn't possess at his age. Nabil asks if we're familiar with Bruno Mars, sharing his enthusiastic fandom. Nabil is as kind and considerate as the adult members of his family and over the course of our stay, we grow quite endeared to him.

Directed by his Mom to essentially shadow us on a regular basis after school, we contest. What teenager wants to be burdened by such a mundane obligation? But he shrugs it off, holding a mirror of gratitude to us, stating that we are affording him the opportunity to practice English. And just as his mother requests, Nabil visits daily to assist with translation, always patient and never revealing that he's tiring of us.

Yasmine, Haja's adult granddaughter, is as kind as she is beautiful. And like Haja, Yasmine possesses a very gentle nature. The family is incredibly proud of her success as a cardiologist. She too speaks fluent English and informs me that when the workday is through, Moroccans customarily spend evenings among family. She invites us to meet her sister, Sophia, the following week. Sophia is a new mother to a baby girl, adopted just one week earlier. Yasmine retrieves her cell phone to share a photo of precious baby Heba.

Around 9PM that evening, we feast on a popular Moroccan dish called bastilla. Vermicelli noodles, vegetables, shrimp, onion, and mild spices are encased in phyllo dough, and it is exceptionally delicious. We sit around a dining table sharing a meal with this amazing family, our new friends. They have become our guardians and allies, sheltering not only our belongings but our hearts. We learn that Haja has reserved our evenings for family gatherings, as she and her daughters have mapped out a dinner schedule for the next two weeks, each ready to host us. Nabil's mother, Lina, declares her plan to make homemade pizza the following night. We are undeserving of this treatment, but feel overwhelming appreciation for it.

Once the meal is finished, we help clear the dishes and retreat to the room lined with couches. Haja and one of her daughters spend the next hour relaxing and chatting with ease. When there's a sudden break in conversation, I follow Haja's gaze, her attention directed to the television. An evening soap opera broadcasts heavy, suspenseful music. Language is no longer a barrier, as the melodramatic scene reveals an irate woman approaching and then smothering her bedridden husband. Careful not to be seen, she slyly drags him to a field, burying his body under the moonlight. Haja is tickled by the spectacle. She laughs and looks at me while pointing to the television, wanting me to share in this entertaining absurdity. For the first time all day, I laugh, unraveling the ball of stress that has been knotted inside me. I laugh at the twist of fate that brought us to Haja, a delightful, kindhearted, loving woman. She does not treat us as strangers or even friends, but family.

Today's reality revealed the precariousness of this process. But returning to Haja's home relieves with a sense of loving protection, something a hotel's concierge could never supply.

As the evening winds down, Russ and I commence to our room. It's the first time we've been alone all day. In the dark of Haja's bedroom, we whisper our growing concerns for this adoption. We check our email and find a new message from Murre sent to all families tethered to the Morocco program. Attached is a document entitled, "What to expect when you arrive in Morocco," and it details an introduction to "your child" upon meeting the orphanage director. Our concerns balloon as we wonder why our experience has been so vastly different.

LAURI M. VELOTTA-RANKIN

## "En Shallah"

A new day brings refreshed perspective and revived hope. With help from the aroma of Haja's dark roast coffee and the warm morning sun, I manage to free myself of lingering doubt. This process is exclusively facilitated by our appointed representative and, like it or not, entirely out of our hands. We simply have to trust our agency and their Moroccan counterpart. So during this two-week stay in Rabat, I vow to relinquish control, abide by Nada's guidance, and absorb our children's remarkable culture to share with them one day.

Haja prepares instant oatmeal with a side of fresh oranges and pastries. I set the table for three and we gather around the small kitchen table for breakfast. While eating, Haja points to a wall clock hung above the doorframe and states the Arabic names of its twelve numbers. As best we can, we repeat each word aloud. She corrects gently when we butcher the name and smiles with encouragement when we get it right.

When required to communicate with someone solely by nonverbal means, it's an unusual but fascinating experience. I'm so impressed and humbled by Haja's kindness that I often find myself holding hands with her to convey my appreciation and rapidly-growing affection.

## SHEER WILLPOWER

Russ and I continually strive to express our gratitude through small gestures like refilling Haja's coffee, helping with the dishes, and purchasing a new coffee pot to replace hers with the broken handle. Our efforts are minimal, practically insignificant in contrast to her benevolence, but we long for her to understand how very thankful we are.

Shortly after breakfast, she turns on the television and channel surfs, settling on a cooking show. Within a few minutes, a commercial airs and our attention is immediately seized:

*The distinct rhythm of a heart monitor.*
*A woman's pain resonances as she struggles through labor.*
*The cries of a newborn overpower a fading heartbeat.*
*It flatlines and the mother falls motionless.*
*The hands of a nurse methodically clean and swaddle the baby in a blanket.*
*In slow motion, the nurse walks down a dark hospital corridor with the baby in her arms.*
*The sunlight shines brighter with each window she passes.*
*The music crescendos as the camera refocuses on an anxious couple.*
*Their faces erupt with joy as she places the baby in the new mother's arms.*
*A family is born.*
*(Fade to black.)*

This is yet another instance where language comprehension isn't needed as we immediately grasp the message of this commercial. It is later explained that a newly-launched campaign promoting domestic adoption was initiated by Morocco's royal family. We wonder if this is playing an active role in the friction we've encountered. The worries I tried to stifle now resurface.

Nada arranges for us to meet our lawyer, Amira, today. She will assist with the adoption paperwork specific to Morocco. Nada leads us to Rabat's Ministry of Justice, where we make our introductions.

Amira is fluent in Arabic and French but we soon realize that she doesn't speak any English. It's another perplexing decision that makes us question the integrity of this process. Yes, we're foreigners unable to speak the local language—but for this significant a matter, why wouldn't Murre ensure we have an English-speaking lawyer? Legal representation is crucial as Amira will guide us through sensitive and cumbersome legal documentation, and we foot the bill for her time.

It's uncomfortable and difficult to muzzle a screaming logic that dictates never signing your name or providing your social security number on a document you cannot read. But our circumstance is atypical and we do not want to present any outward signs of hesitation. We could easily offend both Nada and Amira, thus jeopardizing our adoption. At this point in time, what is our alternative? So we silence our concerns, rely exclusively on Nada's translation, and repeatedly sign the literal dotted line.

We consent to have our names checked against various international databases that scan for criminal records. Amira informs us that the police report is valid for the next two months, but if we aren't matched with children within this timeframe, it will expire. The clock is officially running.

Nada communicates our difficulties with the Rabat orphanage director to Amira, and after they converse for several minutes without translation, Nada declares her desire to travel to an orphanage in Salé, about twenty minutes north of Rabat. Amira is familiar with its orphanage director and suspects we'd have better luck there. It is clearly becoming a game of hunt-and-peck, but we are making progress with our paperwork and trust in Nada's abilities. The following day is Friday, the Muslim Holy Day, and with court on Monday, Nada opts to travel to Salé on Tuesday, "en shallah."

## SHEER WILLPOWER

A common Moroccan expression, spoken often by Nada, is "en shallah." Its English translation is "God-willing," and she typically tacks it onto the end of select sentences. God is incorporated into various facets of everyday life in Morocco and I find myself entranced by these overt words of reverence. But Nada's use of it soon begins to reek and reveal itself as a disclaimer instead of a prayer.

LAURI M. VELOTTA-RANKIN

# Train to Marrakesh

*"Exercise caution in your business affairs, for the world is full of trickery. But let this not blind you to what virtue there is. Many persons strive for high ideals and everywhere life is full of heroism."* —Max Ehrmann (Desiderata)

With no appointments scheduled that Friday, we opt to give Haja reprieve for the long weekend. We adore our host family and their outstanding hospitality, but the adoption-related developments have us tightly wound. I feel like the plate of a light switch with a screw continually being forced in too deeply, ready to crack. And the analogy is appropriate, as each passing day exposes a crack in the process, dimming our hopes. Seeking time to decompress and clear our heads, we decide to travel by train about five hours south to the city of Marrakesh.

The lyrics to the old song *Marrakesh Express* (by Crosby, Stills, and Nash) is ironically analogous with our sentiments: "Traveling the train through clear Moroccan skies... hope the days that lie ahead bring us back to where they've led."

Once aboard, I settle into my seat and enjoy the scenery passing outside my window. Our travel takes us southward and inland, and I find the landscape unexpected and mesmerizing. Sparse patches of lone bushes amidst dry, brown landscape transition to swollen emerald hills speckled with shepherds herding flocks. Uninhabited land spreads for miles while homes are clustered within towering red-clay ramparts. The scenes rushing by are ripped from the pages of magazines promoting foreign travel.

Some villages divulge their wealth with exquisitely detailed construction while others have visibly been battered by time and neglect. However, the swing of affluence's pendulum is unaffected by one ubiquitous commonality: satellite dishes.

Roofs of apartment buildings are overrun by enormous grey discs directed skyward. And thanks to our time spent with Haja and her family, we gain insight into popular television shows: French cartoons, Moroccan cooking shows, and dubbed-over Spanish soap operas, all temporarily pausing for the animation (reminiscent of a hypnotic screensaver from the nineties) issuing the call to prayer. The television consistently has an audience. Similar to many American households, TV holds a central role of entertainment in the Moroccan family.

Our train makes numerous stops and I enjoy people-watching out the window. At one station, our car rests directly in front of a family of four. Seated on a bench, parents affectionately observe their son playing a game of peek-a-boo with his little brother who is overcome by fits of laughter. Mom and Dad smile softly, contentedly. It is a sweet and serene moment to observe, but I am acutely aware of the fact that I am watching from behind the glass. I am not a participant but merely a witness. I ache to share similar moments with my own family but sense it slipping away. It actually isn't as gentle as slipping implies. It is being yanked from my raw hands as I desperately clutch it with all my might.

Nearly five hours later, we arrive in Marrakesh, bathed in sunlight and modernity. High rise buildings, flashing billboards, and ample street traffic ignite the city. We descend the train onto a wide concrete platform and walk towards the station.

When seeking lodging, online research, reviews, and calls have led us to a converted home centered around a roofless courtyard called a riad. This riad is situated within the walled inner city of Marrakesh. Russ spoke with the affable owner who casually stated that we would be met at the train station and driven to the riad. He did not require a credit card number or even full name to reserve the room.

Among the hordes of people who've just disembarked the train, we notice a man standing motionlessly along the platform. Dressed in casual attire, he holds a small white sign with the name of our riad scrolled across it in blue ink. Unsure if this is meant for us, we cautiously approach and introduce ourselves. He greets us kindly, shaking both our hands, and reaches down to unburden me of my luggage. We follow him to his vehicle and he opens the car's back door, gesturing for us to climb inside.

It is another instance where logic dictates (*shouts!*) not to enter a stranger's car that presents no markings of its employer or visible license as a cabbie—because this is not a taxi or car service. Rather, it is evident that we are about to ride in this man's personal vehicle. But the riad owner specifically stated that transportation would be provided, and we remind ourselves that we're visiting a foreign land with customs that differ from our own. So with the scales tipping towards a copacetic scenario, we thank him and squeeze into the backseat.

Reaching the perimeter of Marrakesh's old city, we all vacate the car and approach the towering rampart enveloping eleven miles of its ancient interior. The wall is like nothing I've ever laid eye upon. It is a superbly impressive monstrosity.

## SHEER WILLPOWER

Our driver waves over a second man who nods in greeting and takes ahold of our luggage. He leads us through an arched, keyhole-shaped doorway carved within the wall granting entrance.

Once we step through, we are instantly transported back in time to a mystical city, its narrow streets scarcely broader than my outstretched arms. The dual sides of this massive rampart present a jaw-dropping juxtaposition. A few steps back, we treaded asphalt and concrete. But now the soles of our shoes connect with stones that hail from the eleventh century.

With bags loaded onto a donkey-drawn cart, our excitement grows with each minute of this astonishing experience. As we trail this four-legged chauffeur, the driver directs our attention to specific shops and restaurants positioned along the slender passage. Every few feet we're taking sharp turns down different alleyways and my directional sense becomes muddled. It is a labyrinth of high-walled, nameless streets and I'm relieved when a map is provided. But even that is disorienting, reminding me of a complex maze my pencil navigated in a *Highlights* magazine as a child.

We're led down a canopied alley sheltering a succession of bejeweled doors. It dead ends at a rich, sapphire blue door bearing no sign or indication of what lies inside. Our driver gives a gentle push, exposing the small door cut from within the frame of the larger one: an *Alice in Wonderland*-eque door-within-a-door. He cautions our step, as it opens several inches above the ground, only rising about five feet high. Walking ahead, he disappears down the long, dimly lit hallway. Another instance of "cross your fingers and hope for the best" challenges us but we obediently follow his lead. As we proceed further, the decorative tiled floor gains visibility and I hear the songs of birds and trickling water ahead—which baffles, because we just left the outdoors.

Adil, the riad owner, warmly greets us while balancing a tray holding a kettle of mint tea and cookies in one steady hand. He guides us to the center atrium housing a garden with trees extending several stories to the open sky above. A fountain along the far wall is accentuated with a series of intricate Moroccan lanterns, illuminating the floor in a confetti of soft hues. The riad is stunning.

He sets the tray down on a small wooden table and the three of us descend onto its matching cushioned chairs. Adil asks about our travels and delivers suggestions for where to venture while in Marrakesh. There is no rush to his words and no obligatory friendliness detected in his demeanor. Adil treats us as invited guests in his home. When he excuses himself to process our stay, Russ and I gush about this exquisite establishment and our congenial host.

By the time we settle into our beautiful and immaculate room, the sun has set and evening arrives. We're excited to explore these surroundings, so we study the map and determine our route through the old city. Before we turn the first corner outside of the riad, Adil is on our heels, calling after us. He apologetically explains the forecast of an impending storm and hands us an umbrella.

The ancient city pulsates with energy. It is dense with pedestrians and shop vendors who spill onto the streets in zealous pursuit of attention. They speak over one another, sometimes waving their arms to garner interest, and I quickly learn that eye contact is perceived as an invitation to engage. Admittedly, it's a bit overwhelming.

An assortment of merchandise is strategically placed in view of passersby: glazed ceramic bowls, silver tea sets, warm shades of spices, silk tunics and pashminas, glossy olives artistically stacked to a precarious peak. With such a wide array of colors, textures, designs, and lighting, it comes as no surprise that this is such a highly photographed metropolis.

## SHEER WILLPOWER

We weave our way to the heart of the old city, Jemaa el-Fna. This marketplace, called a "souk," swells with a large center square rife with food vendors, entertainers, and foot traffic. Smoke from outdoor grills fills the air with alluring aromas, while various acoustical performances compete with one another and the drone of the growing crowd. A corner café exhibits its food within lighted glass displays, an assortment of alluring dishes.* Enticed, we enter and sit at the only vacant table immediately inside the front door. As permitted in many local restaurants, we find ourselves sucking in the fumes of smokers seated around us, so before a waiter draws near, we relinquish our table in search of an alternative dining option.

Back outside, we're drawn to an enormous tent floating above a series of long wooden picnic tables situated around a display of skewered meats and vibrant vegetables. Contained in oversized bowls, the produce is piled to gravity-challenging heights. The grill master is engulfed in smoke, though he doesn't choke or seem bothered by it as he furiously and skillfully tosses meat on and off the fire. Customers are hunched over plates filled with mouthwatering meals. Russ and I sit across from one another along a bench and are soon joined by fellow diners. A waiter directs us to select our meat and vegetables from the stand, so we point at various bowls while he scribbles on a small notepad and hastily departs. Shortly thereafter, we feast like ravenous animals for a total of thirty dollars. Grilled vegetables, couscous, and a variety of meats, seasoned with spices foreign to my palate—it is one of the best meals I've ever consumed.

---

* Six weeks later, the smoky café in the main souk was decimated in a terrorist attack when a nail-laden bomb tragically killed seventeen innocents. We were stunned and saddened when we recognized its destroyed exterior on the morning news. https://en.wikipedia.org/wiki/2011_Marrakesh_bombing

We then explore the busy square, but nighttime provokes a new determination in vendors aggressively nipping at heels. We're followed by several shopkeepers shouting a succession of plunging prices, like an auctioneer in reverse. "La shukran" (Arabic for "no thank you") is apparently understood as "Give me a better offer."

The cold drizzle begins to fall and we are weary from the long day, so we shelter our heads under Adil's umbrella and walk back to the riad.

The following morning, we venture to a quiet shop near our riad. Lamps of shimmering brass with elaborate cutouts hang from the ceiling while mixed-metal merchandise line the walls at varying heights. Rasheed, a lanky and gregarious young man, welcomes us with arms extended, proud to present his goods. He doesn't bait with high-pressure sales and we're soon engaged in a friendly exchange. Drawn to a particular tea set, he offers a variety of accompanying silver trays, kettles, and a kaleidoscopic of colored, curvy glasses. We admire the lovely collections and select our preferences. Our inquiry into sugar bowls results in a moment's pause, and then Rasheed casually announces that he'll be back in a few minutes. We watch him walk out the front door of his one-manned shop, hop onto his moped, and with a rev of the engine, shrink from sight.

We laugh in disbelief that we've just been left there alone, and awkwardly stand in place, unsure what to do. Thankfully, Rasheed is gone for no more than three minutes. He's toting a plastic grocery bag clanging with an assortment of sugar bowls retrieved from another vendor. Yes, he's a businessman trying to make a sale, but I don't care if they're tarnished and deformed, I will buy one. I'm determined because he didn't treat us with the distrust we confronted so frequently this past week—and right now, that means everything to me.

We make our purchases from Rasheed's shop and ask if he can recommend a particular place for pashminas. We would like to find

## SHEER WILLPOWER

one for Haja. He once again vacates his store, but this time, we are in tow. Leading us down the road, he brings us into a small shop where pashminas line the walls from floor to ceiling. Thanking him again, we shake his hand goodbye, and he leaves us to browse the rainbow of silks.

While we comb through the rich colors, a man approaches declaring, "Ah, sounds like Americans!" We affirm his assumption and discover he's an American dentist providing impoverished children with free dental care. In under a week, his team has worked in the mouths of over six hundred kids. Learning the purpose of our travel, he advises we bring our children to a dentist immediately upon our return to the states. Quite honestly, the condition of their teeth is one of the least of my concerns, but I appreciate the insight. We praise his wonderful work and wish him luck with the remainder of his trip.

The evening before departing Marrakesh, we pass Rasheed's shop and see him standing at its entrance. We approach to say our goodbyes but he takes ahold of Russ's arm and excitedly states, "I have something for you!" Rasheed ushers us inside, snatching two candle holders from his counter. He carefully wraps them in paper and thanks us for our business. While expressing appreciation for the opportunity to practice his English, Rasheed hands us the gift. His act of kindness is so pure and decent, and I'm touched beyond words. I want to embrace him in a hug while breaking down in tears, and relate the difficulties of the past week. But instead, I thank him, taking ahold of his one hand between my two and lightly squeezing, hoping this properly conveys my appreciation.

There are many adages about small gestures resulting in impactful gratitude, and this occurrence is exemplary. But Rasheed does not stand alone in our admiration. Adil is deserving of another mention as well. Perhaps his peaceful manner and thoughtfulness are standard business practices, but we were desperate for reprieve. These two men, utter strangers, treated us with respect and kindheartedness during one of the most emotionally-charged chapters of our lives.

**SHEER WILLPOWER**

## Sophia's Story

Haja's granddaughter, Sophia, had adopted a newborn baby girl the week prior to our arrival in Morocco. Haja and Yasmine had planned a visit with them the evening of our return from Marrakesh.

Under a different set of circumstances, or perhaps earlier in our trip, we would have been honored and delighted to meet them both. Successful adoption stories had always fueled our excitement and anticipation. But after a week of witnessing our adoption spin violently out of control, we honestly dreaded this particular introduction. It was unintentional salt to a very fresh wound, and emotional fragility was spreading like a virus, diseasing my well-being. I feared that seeing Sophia lovingly cradle her new daughter would break me.

But Haja was so proud and keen to have us meet her granddaughter and great-granddaughter, and the family had already arranged for a car to deliver us. It was too late to retreat and not wanting to offend our gracious host, we literally and figuratively buckled ourselves in for the ride.

The story of Sophia's adoption was quick and uncomplicated, and we assumed various details had been omitted for the ease of translation.

As it was explained to us, many unwed mothers provide false names and slip from their hospital beds shortly after giving birth, leaving behind their newborns. Sophia and her husband had added their names to a hospital registry of families seeking to adopt these abandoned babies. The week prior to our arrival in Morocco, they received a phone call from the hospital. A newborn had been deserted and they were asked if they would like to adopt her. Two days were allotted for consideration. The elated couple scrambled to gather the typical new-parent essentials.

Three days prior, Sophia was a working woman coping with fertility-related difficulties. Several cycles of in-vitro fertilization resulted in tragic loss with two miscarriages. But life changed in an instant—more precisely, a week. She's now a blissful, bleary-eyed mother of a newborn daughter, kindly welcoming us into her home.

Sophia is an articulate and successful Moroccan beauty in her early thirties. The apartment is immaculate, luxuriously decorated with milky marble-tiled floors, textured wallpaper, and lush furnishings. Stylish accents are muted in a sophisticated color palette of lavender and deep grey. The kitchen is outfitted in sleek stainless steel appliances and granite countertops, rivaling upscale model homes in the states. A pair of sliding glass doors opens to an outdoor balcony overlooking the setting sun and the elephant exhibit from a neighboring zoo.

Voices are hushed because baby Heba is asleep in a nearby bedroom. My insides settle with this news and I desperately wish for her to peacefully slumber throughout the duration of our stay.

Greeting Yasmine, we embrace in a warm hug before sitting, and she kindly assists with translation. Introductions are made and we are steered towards a couch. The women position themselves around us and we meet Sabrine, Haja's sister, who is mother to both Sophia and

## SHEER WILLPOWER

Yasmine. Sabrine rises and places tray tables at our knees, followed by plates, napkins, and glasses for tea. The large coffee table is overrun with platefuls of decadent goodies and my resolve crumbles as I eye the neatly stacked Moroccan cookies. Fragrant mint tea is poured for all in attendance. Hand gestures, directed from the treats to plates, suggest we begin. Russ and I modestly select three small cookies each, but Sabrine good-naturedly seizes a handful more, piling them on each of our plates. Laughter erupts and we thank her, "Shukran, Sabrine!" Yasmine passes along our appreciation for the invitation as well as compliments on the beauty of Sophia's home and the abundance of food.

We turn our attention to Sophia and congratulate her on Heba. We inquire about Heba with a series of common questions new parents often receive. She then narrates the story about Heba's arrival, and to our surprise, there is no deviation from what was already explained to us. Astounded, we can hardly fathom the simplicity. We detail the arduous adoption system in the US, and how adopting overseas has been challenging as well. Through speaking with Sophia and family, we discover that Moroccan citizenship is the golden ticket that expedites adoption procedures with little fuss. This is something we do not possess.

Sophia and Yasmine momentarily sneak away and soon return, excitedly informing us that the baby is now awake. My heart races as everyone jumps to their feet and ushers us along, eager for us to meet this child.

We're led down a hallway towards the back of the home and I struggle to control my erratic breathing. I can't meet Russ's eyes but I feel them on me. Terrified I'll cry, I warn myself it will gravely insult this wonderful family. I never would have imagined I'd be so apprehensive to meet a baby.

We enter the master bedroom and Sophia gently scoops the silent newborn from her crib. She holds her at an angle, displaying Heba with pride.

Heba is an Islamic name that beautifully translates to "gift from God." And she is just that. Heba is *magnificent*. Sophia graciously offers Heba to me and my grief dissipates as I swell with humility. I'm deeply honored that my holding her is meaningful to this family. I softly cradle this newborn in my arms, her tiny body's warmth descending upon me. Her deep, dark eyes are directed at the mass that is Russ standing beside me. She intensely stares at him, absorbed in his cadence as he tenderly speaks to her, and we all laugh in acknowledgement of the sweet moment.

Back at Haja's home and tucked into bed, I search the dark in introspective thought. I feel shame that I hadn't wanted to meet Heba, and I wonder what was infecting my emotions. Was I so convinced our adoption would fail that I was souring to others who reached success? Was this process chipping away my strength? Had I become so unnerved that I preemptively molded a protective coating, hardening my emotions? I couldn't quite sort out the answers to these questions. Perhaps it was a bitter blend of each. But the ultimate paradox is that my fear was quelled, my heart softened, and I received comfort the moment a seven-pound baby, this "gift from God," was placed in my arms.

And with a storybook ending, three weeks after welcoming baby Heba, Sophia discovers that she is pregnant.

## Judgment Day

*"No one can make you feel inferior without your consent." —Eleanor Roosevelt*

We are expected in Rabat's Court of Minors Monday morning for a hearing to obtain guardianship of the children, a critical element of this process. Leaving Morocco without it would essentially disqualify us, crippling our adoption endeavor. Although that prospect could find me running to the bathroom with dry heaves, Murre assures that this hearing is simply a formality. Lilith provides the following guidance about our court appearance: "The judge will ask you a variety of questions including names, places of residence, employer and date of birth. You may be asked some other questions as well." Although her details on the proceedings are vague, her counsel on one specific issue is unequivocal. She confirms that I packed a scarf to cover my head while in court. "Yes," I reassure her. "I brought three."

However, when I mention the scarf to Nada the day before our hearing, she firmly advises against its necessity. Not wanting to offend the woman directly facilitating our adoption, I heed Nada's words and instead, conservatively pull my hair back into a low bun.

The gravity of this hearing finds us arriving half an hour earlier than Nada had scheduled, so we linger on the exterior stairs of the courthouse. Russ is outfitted in a charcoal-colored suit with an unadorned maroon tie while I pair a tweed pant suit in a neutral shade with low-profile heels. When Nada approaches, she's clad in tight, low-rise jeans and an untucked button down shirt. Unfamiliar with the social norms and customs of the Moroccan courts, I digest her relaxed attire as an additional signal that this is, indeed, an informal hearing.

When we enter the courthouse, the atrium is lit with activity and the conversational hum of its occupants bounce echoes off the stone walls. But I instantly observe a glaring distinction, as every woman we pass has a covered head. And I'm incredulous as I watch Nada casually pluck a green scarf from her purse, draping it over her own. I am the only female with exposed hair and can't help but feel the weight of stares upon it.

Nada directs us to an office where she speaks Arabic to its two female inhabitants. They too wear scarves. When their business is complete, Nada leads us to a bench outside the courtroom's closed door where we await Amira. Nada will provide our adoption paperwork and translate when questions are directed to us while Amira spearheads all legal inquiries. Several moments later, Amira arrives dressed in a dark pant suit. She casts a quizzical glance at Nada's jeans and they engage in a conversation that is not afforded translation.

Once summoned inside, I survey the room. It bears a resemblance to the courtroom I found myself in to contest a speeding ticket years prior. My energy is nervous excitement, but I remind myself that this hearing is merely a formality.

The judge approaches his bench, elevated a few feet above the room. Tall and slender, he appears to be in his early sixties. Wire-rimmed glasses cling low on his nose and the corners of his mouth are turned down with wrinkles rippled around it, as if this countenance has been permanently etched into his skin from years of practice. He presents a stoic and tense expression. I convince myself that his demeanor will soften once he learns the reason for our appearance.

We are seeking the judge's approval for our adoption to advance, but we had not anticipated the need to defend ourselves.

With a furrowed brow, he begins his discourse, delivering questions in a highly vexed tone. As Nada launches into translation, he interrupts with raised voice. Arabic words flow from Nada's flustered mouth in an apologetic tone with reverent gestures. The exchange is short and his eyes turn down as he silently thumbs through the papers before him. While his attention is occupied, Nada brings us up to speed in a hushed tone. But before she can finish, he speaks with attention fixed on me. I look to Nada for translation and he erupts, finally revealing his English tongue as he angrily demands, "Why are you here? Who *are* you?" She informs him that she represents us and is helping to find the children.

Suddenly, Nada snaps her head away from him, leaning in to Russ and me. An urgent, imperative declaration rushes across her lips as she tells us to ensure we *do not* mention our agency's involvement in this adoption. Instead, she directs us to state that we've connected with her on our own.

My stomach lurches into a frenzy of somersaults. We don't understand what the hell is happening and why we're being instructed to lie.

He returns to his native tongue and permitting Nada's translation, commences with an onslaught of questions that feel akin to an interrogation. He wants to know why we are seeking adoption. He asks how our families feel about this decision. He requests information about our jobs, monthly incomes, and the number of floors and bedrooms in our home, as Murre had informed. But their guidance of "some other questions" fails to prepare us for the emotional intrusion of what follows.

He inquires about biological children and when we reply that we don't have any, he asks if we are "unable." We explain that we cannot conceive naturally and assume the answer will suffice, ending an awkward line of questioning. But he continues to pry, asking *why*. And then a pointed finger emerges, swinging between Russ and me, as he seeks to identify the culprit of this faulty biology.

Cultural differences permit ample latitude with questions, but he makes these insensitive intrusions with no measure of decorum. We are not on trial for a crime yet we're treated like suspects mounting our defense. It is yet another instance of baffling scrutiny. I am so rattled by this line of questioning that I clench my hands together, securing them in my lap so he can't see them shake.

I feel humiliated, unnerved, and stripped of dignity.

But this antagonistic assault is not over. Before reaching a verdict on our guardianship, he stares us down with spiteful intimidation. His eyes dart to my husband's face and hold, like he's initiating a staring contest. For no less than thirty seconds he locks eyes with Russ, not speaking a single word. The room is silent and out of fear or inability, I remain motionless. When he's satisfied with whatever was gained from this tactic, he offers no reprieve as he turns a penetrating glare on me. Unsure if I should avert my eyes or meet his gaze, I offer the slightest, pleading smile, the nonverbal wave of a white flag. I wish I could understand what he wants or expects from us, but I'm desperate for him to know that we are pure-intentioned and deeply yearn to parent orphaned children. But my smile is met with actionless rejection. I'm terrified that he'll deny us and this fear seeps into my legs as they begin to tremble under the courtroom table.

## SHEER WILLPOWER

Our facilitator and lawyer may have convinced him to check the box necessary to advance this adoption, but they left us vulnerable to unanticipated, unabashed antagonism. We vacate the courtroom feeling not only wounded, but freshly alarmed. He is the second person holding an authoritative role in aiding our adoption who has reacted with distrust and outright abrasion.

*Why?*

We later learn this was Nada's first involvement with the Rabat court system. She tells us about the recent passing of a judge who easily permitted adoptions to foreigners, while this new judge has a tendency to reject them. *Reject* them! I feel the transparency of this revelation. Many thoughts fight for occupancy on my tongue, but the relief she expects me to feel is not among them.

Nada commits another blunder. We had asked what we should bring with us to court, and with a wave of her hand, she stated that there was nothing. Before departing Haja's house that morning, Russ decided to pocket a copy of our dossier and passports. It was no surprise when a clerk asked for our passports as we entered the courtroom that morning. I believe the hearing would have been canceled without them.

The entire occurrence had been an astounding mess: my lack of head covering, Nada's casual attire, the passport requirement, and the shocking resistance from the judge. Nada had seriously underestimated the magnitude of this process and our confidence in her was crumbling.

Nada informs us that Rania will receive the judge's official approval letter two days before we depart Morocco. Anticipating its legality will provide Rania reassurance, Nada recommends we make another visit to the orphanage after its receipt. She does not envision any other obstacles will emerge and is hopeful we will meet some of the children.

**SHEER WILL**POWER

# One Last Try

*"The women whom I love and admire for their strength and grace did not get that way because shit worked out. They got that way because shit went wrong and they handled it. They handled it in a thousand different ways on a thousand different days, but they handled it. Those women are my superheroes."* —Elizabeth Gilbert

Wednesday morning, we meet Nada with hopes of hearing positive news about the Salé orphanage she planned to visit yesterday. But Nada never made the trip, citing a handful of obscure reasons.

Instead, she informs us that today we'll visit the Rabat orphanage again. Furnished with judicial approval, she's confident we'll receive a warmer welcome. We leave Morocco tomorrow and are desperate for some indication of forward progress.

Again, Nada enters Rania's office alone, leaving us to nervously pace the hall. Within a few minutes, she sticks her head out and motions us inside. Russ and I respectfully greet Rania in Arabic, and descend onto two metal chairs. We're not seated at a close distance meant for communication, but rather awkwardly exposed in the room's center, as if exhibited for visual inspection. Rania sits shrouded by her desk, while we are on full-display.

Nada had suggested that the judge's letter would soften Rania's demeanor as well as permit access to the orphanage, but neither happens. For a second time, she will not allow us to see any children or even volunteer the remainder of our last day at the orphanage. She speaks abruptly with the body language of indifference, and Nada turns to us with translation. Before she even speaks, I know the news is not favorable. Rania believes we should seek a single child instead of two, adding that we could adopt again with the undefined timetable of "later."

A few days prior, Murre had updated a requirement for Moroccan adoptions. Two mandatory visits to Morocco had increased to three, totaling approximately four weeks in-country. Attaining a four-week absence from a job is difficult for any working professional, but two separate adoptions, as Rania suggests, necessitates a total of eight weeks. The cost also skyrockets with additional weeks of accommodations and food allowances, and now a staggering six flights to northern Africa. The ballooning cost would not end there. The replication of government and administrative paperwork, either eliminated or discounted when adopting two at once, would be squashed. This wasn't an inconvenience, this was a financial and professional impossibility.

One of the most significant factors in deciding to adopt from Morocco was the approval to adopt two children at once, and now we are being robbed of this too.

Deviations from established requirements are essentially protocol in international adoption, and we hadn't expected personal immunity. But this ride is veering wildly off-course. We are at the mercy of these adoption authorities to assist our journey, but instead, we are relentlessly treated with utter apathy or contempt, often both.

## SHEER WILLPOWER

At that precise moment in Rania's office, emotional fatigue and defeat settle into the marrow of my every bone and a devastating realization instantly sets: *we are chasing ghosts*. I look into my husband's eyes. His kind and mild-mannered temperament have been visibly replaced by raw anguish and quiet rage. I collapse under the weight of this powerlessness and begin to weep openly.

Understanding that we need time to process this setback, Nada recommends we reunite later that day. Before parting, she asks that we bring copies of our dossier with us. She devises a plan to distribute them to orphanage directors in several other Moroccan cities. "I like to have my hand in many pots," she reassures.

When we return to Haja's home, we find her contentedly watching daytime television. As usual, she greets us warmly and I sit beside her on the couch. We can't communicate, but we don't even need to. Being in Haja's presence melts my stress. She offers protective sheltering, and just knowing her enriches my life. I have grown to love her like a member of my own family.

Sitting with Haja, I open my laptop to email family and close friends with this latest update. And then I hear the blip. The commercial promoting domestic adoption airs.

I ache to return home.

That evening, we meet Nada for the last time. Russ and I had accumulated two pages of questions scribbled on a notepad with hopes of her restoring our spirits. We still have faith in Nada and believe she is our ally.

We had been rerouted to Rabat because of an increased wait in Meknes, so we ask if she could inquire about our current positioning.

Lilith said Meknes is a successful orphanage for Americans, so even with the extended wait, we wonder if it is best to focus our efforts there instead. This is when we're dealt another blow: when Nada redirected us to Rabat, our dossier was *removed* from Meknes, where it had been in queue for a period of six months. We were starting over in Rabat, with our dossier placed behind every family already in their system.

We were called to Rabat with the assumption that our dossier had reached the top of the stack. All adoption agencies mirror this step: a call to travel signifies that you've been matched with a child. But as we discovered at the end of our visit, Rania had never even laid eyes on our dossier until we were seated in her office.

Disillusioned, we express frustration with Nada for the first time, and she smashes open another revelation. She confides the precise reason for these extended waits: a baby girl. She tells us that she explicitly asked Lilith to stop accepting dossiers from families seeking girls, as they are often sought by Moroccan families and few remain in orphanages. But despite her message, she continues to receive these requests from Murre.

We made the preference for a boy and a girl because Lilith had told us that both genders were readily available. Yet we are learning about the difficulty of adopting girls while in Morocco, with paralyzing awareness that our legal paperwork (submitted last year to both domestic and foreign governments) indicates the selection of each gender.

With this admission, we realize we have just spun our wheels on a trip taken in vain. We now know that the work we did with Amira will expire before a match is made.

The only true accomplishment we have while in-country is getting a peek behind the curtain where we uncover a stringent aversion to foreign adoptions, a malfunctioning adoption process, and a severe disconnect between our adoption agency and their own representative.

And with that looming over us, we prepare to return home.

# Farewell, Haja

*"Family not only need to consist of merely those whom we share blood, but also for those whom we'd give blood." —Charles Dickens*

The hardest part about being in Morocco was feeling like suspects subjected to the bright fluorescent lights of a criminal investigation. But the hardest part about leaving Morocco is saying goodbye to Haja.

Our final hugs are a bittersweet moment. I can't wait to be home, but parting from Haja hurts my heart. Her son would call often to check in with us and on that final day, he told me, "She's really going to miss you guys." We disrupted her life for two weeks, encroaching on her space and altogether eliminating her privacy. And yet, she's sad to see us go.

Haja believes that pursuing an adoption in her country is a thing of integrity and was simply honoring our efforts with accommodations. She hasn't regarded her role with the same degree of virtuousness as we have, and she'd likely scoff at any praise and attention I give to this aspect of our travels.

But I really can't help myself.

## SHEER **WILL**POWER

I have struggled with the right fitting of words to express my sentiments for this woman and her family. We expected a room in which to sleep and perhaps a few meals. Instead, we were the undeserving recipients of a remarkable family who supported us throughout this entire ordeal. They were unguarded, effortlessly welcoming us without reservation, and the kindness they showered upon us fills me with unmatched humility. They epitomize the rare authenticity and pure goodness that seeks nothing in return. It's worth restating: we were strangers to them but were never treated as such.

Without a common language, there was a heavy reliance on exaggerated facial expressions and miming with hand gestures, hoping the message and its intent was understood. There were plenty of times Haja rattled off a string of sentences in her native tongue followed by visual cues that were just lost on me. I was never very adept at charades. Sometimes I feigned comprehension, opting to nod or smile instead of exasperating her with apologetic looks of confusion, and I'm fairly sure she too employed this method. Despite these limitations, I always felt an unspoken closeness with Haja. And not only did I feel comfortable, I was often compelled to lovingly touch her, whether it was with a hug or holding her hand. Even in photos, our tilted heads meet or hands connect.

And then suddenly, I must say goodbye to the person who sheltered us with loving generosity. Her family helps translate, but I hope she can sense the sincerity and our depths of love and appreciation.

Quite unexpectedly, Haja has become a revered mother-figure to us both.

On our ride to Casablanca's airport, Russ and I laugh as we recall our initial apprehension about staying with Adam's mother. With deep nods, we agree that when in her presence there is a mysterious air of holiness. Haja is an instrument of peace, who reverently and quietly serves God through the gentility of her actions. The greatest benevolence we've known illuminated itself in one of the most unpredicted places and unsuspecting forms: that of a small Muslim woman with whom we didn't share a language.

I look out the cab's window and watch the bustle of Rabat race by as we travel out of the city. Releasing a deep breath, I allow the escape of the past two weeks' stress knowing that we did the best we could with tightly bound hands. Despite the uncertainty swirling around our adoption, one thing is cemented in my heart: I am forever grateful for the gift of knowing Haja.

# The Blame Game

The airport taxi approaches our street and settles in our driveway. My feet hit the asphalt before the vehicle is even shifted into park. Though we left Morocco with more questions than when we began, our travels have finally concluded and the mere sight of our home is medicinal. Opening the front door, I inhale deeply, breathing in the familiar, comforting smell that only home can provide. We were away for a mere two weeks, but it somehow feels closer to a year.

I can't wait to gently tip my dog over and stroke his soft belly as his tail whacks the floor with delight. The thought of sleeping in our own bed is perfection. I think about melting into the mattress beneath a mass of cozy blankets and not waking for three days. Switching on the television, even if it's only for the ambient noise, makes me swoon with pleasure. I want to feel the hot water of my own shower and rip open a fresh pack of Twizzlers. I have never felt so happy to resume the often unappreciated routine of everyday life.

Although home nourishes our souls, it cannot ease the concern of our hearts. We are worn and tattered with shaky confidence in our adoption's success.

After a shower and trip to the grocery store, I am very content to stand at the stove and cook an early meal that evening. I watch out the window as Russ ascends the basement stairs to the backyard. He walks over to the newly planted maple tree and makes several slow, inspecting revolutions around its base.

When he returns inside, I ask what he thinks about our property's newest addition. Russ's voice is laced with disappointment. "Its branches were probably bound too long," he says. The nursery's maple trees were bundled when Russ made the selection, and despite their newly found freedom, the tree's limbs remain compact and directed skyward. The tree was frozen in a personified protective pose. We wondered how long it would take for it to relax its branches and discover liberation.

The following Tuesday, Lilith emails that she's "dying to hear" from us, so we prepare and send a lengthy breakdown of our trip, including a list of tips we hope can help the many families standing behind us in line. Lilith replies, "This is priceless!!!!!!!!!!!!!!!! I want to work this into a travel guide as it is 100% what every family must hear and must agree to. I am so proud of you both."

Having her attention, we take this opportunity to detail our concern about being matched with Sarah, the young girl with Down syndrome, as well as Rania's suggestion about adopting the children separately.

Lilith refers to the match with Sarah as "mind blowing and wholly inappropriate," but offers nothing further, as if she is powerless to address this with the orphanage director or even seek an understanding from Nada. Whether it was intentional or spontaneous, it required at least the gesture of an attempted remedy. It was too late for us, but could serve as a valuable clarification or advanced warning for those who follow. Instead, we're seemingly expected to be solely placated by her strong words of dismay.

Regarding Rania's suggestion of adopting individually, she merely suggests that Nada will "remind the director" that we're planning to adopt both children at the same time. It is too passive a statement, as if a minor caveat in the process versus a main artery of our decision to adopt from Morocco. We are just one of many families in this adoption program who selected Morocco because of the allowance to adopt two children concurrently due to the prohibitive cost of two separate adoptions. Lilith spoke of the Morocco program's popularity for this exact reason. Additionally, Murre facilitated a list serve for families within this program to communicate, so we knew many others were in pursuit of two children as well. Rania's statement would have sent a ripple of alarm to Lilith's other clients.

Her reply is baffling. An empathetic relative can state that, but not the director responsible for facilitating the matching of families with orphaned children. Our trepidation is now elevated to a "code red." Rania's suggestion is equally as distressing as Lilith's flippant response.

Lilith's ability to distance herself from these issues abroad is a worry that extends beyond Russ and me. I developed a friendship over email and phone calls with a woman awaiting a child in the same Morocco program. Patricia is a cancer survivor on a quest for motherhood. She had traveled to meet her infant son just over two months prior to our trip. Omar was living in an orphanage a few hours south of Rabat. Patricia had been told that she'd be called to return to Morocco in a few weeks, but began to panic when those weeks stretched into months. While we were in Rabat, Lilith emailed her stating "the baby is sick" with no further elaboration. Bewildered that the information was so vague, and desperate to garner more, Patricia agreed to pay Nada $200 to visit Omar and an additional $400 required for his medical examination. She couldn't fathom why Lilith would send an email devoid of details, which would inherently result in alarm. Wasn't it her duty to extract more and protect the families she served?

And when Patricia learned about the additional required trip abroad, an unexpected four-figured cost, she was sick with worry over the sudden financial burden. I would venture to guess that every family attached to this program shared these sentiments.

While in Rabat, Russ and I had witnessed peaceful protests, activists pursuing political reformation of the king's power. And we couldn't help but feel a parallel to our own repression: our protest has been carefully and delicately delivered, but it fell upon deaf ears.

Nada was leaving the country for a four-week vacation just prior to the expiration of our police and judicial approvals. She had suggested we contact Lilith a month after our return from Rabat so she could update us on the orphanages who received copies of our dossier. She also planned to apprise us of our placement on the Rabat orphanage's waitlist.

Not permitted to correspond with Nada directly, we email Lilith asking if she could seek these answers. Lilith obliges and pastes Nada's reply in an email to us. In Nada's broken English, she states that she spoke with one additional orphanage director who agreed that "it's slow." She does not elaborate or mention distributing our dossier. She did, however, add that we hadn't moved up the Rabat waitlist.

Her reply was two sentences long.

The only achievement our two weeks in Rabat delivered was the execution of these two sets of documents. Aware of their impending expiration dates, Lilith contributes nothing to this content. She doesn't address them or recommend "next steps." She doesn't offer any semblance of explanation or make an effort to ease the worry that saturates our email. With this update from Nada, didn't Lilith wonder about the purpose of our two weeks in Morocco? Wasn't she concerned on the behalf of us and the many families who would follow? Didn't she too have questions? We were her clients but she failed to be our advocate.

Aside from Lilith's apparent indifference, Nada didn't complete the one task she vowed to fulfill: the distribution of our dossier to additional orphanages. Though "It's no problem" was a phrase she repeatedly and confidently declared, it evidently *was* a problem. We were inexplicably shackled to an orphanage whose director regarded us with disdain and suspicion. Despite the number of infants in their care and Lilith's claim that Morocco had a quick turnaround time, our placement on their waitlist hadn't budged. There was no fathomable way we would meet the Moroccan-imposed deadlines. Our trip was in vain. It was a monumental waste of valuable time and precious money.

Lilith assures us that Nada knew our dossier had to remain exclusively in Rabat. This time, we didn't ingest this as another miscommunication. We informed her that couldn't have been Nada's understanding, as she specifically requested our extra dossier copies for the explicit purpose of leaving them with additional orphanage directors. We reported the account with thorough detail: meeting Nada at a café the day prior to our departure, the five dossier copies fastened with binder clips passed over our small table and into Nada's hands, the accordion folder we gave her to better transport them since she only carried a small purse. There was no misinterpretation of this transaction. No disclaimers were stated, no apprehensions offered. Her promise was not even mitigated with an "en shallah." She simply presented this as our next move, confidently declaring, "I like to have my hand in many pots."

Lilith's reply to this is the equivalent of a shoulder shrug. "She's too good of a salesman," my mom's initial warning about her rings in my ears, with the piercing trill of a school fire alarm from the eighties. The round, red metal shell hung high on a wall, being repeatedly pounded by its small hammer. The concern that is failing to give rise to Lilith about Nada is now rapidly percolating inside me about Lilith. Its presence is too intense to ignore.

We can no longer deny the discrepancies and problematic inaction of this agency. Russ and I begin to articulate our doubts to one another, questioning if this adoption will ever come to fruition. Speaking those words aloud horrifies and sickens me.

Feeling that the current atmosphere of our adoption is extremely unstable, we decide our peaceful protest must intensify to gain traction. Together, Russ and I compose an email to Lilith. We sit on it for a day and then revisit the message again. We edit separately, compare notes, and decide on a final version. We want to ensure we are direct with our questions and firm about getting answers, while still remaining optimistic about this process. We feel like we've struck that balance, and with bated breath, I press "send."

SHEER WILLPOWER

# Disposed

*"There comes a time when the bubble of ego is popped and you can't get the ground back for an extended period of time. Those times, when you absolutely cannot get it back together, are the most rich and powerful times in our lives."* —Pema Chödrön

Addressing a multitude of issues in our email to Lilith, we begin by asking why our dossier wasn't distributed to additional orphanages as Nada had promised.

She replies, "Despite Nada's assurance, she had not thought to confirm this with other orphanages... while it may have worked before, it may not now as Nada continues to update us as she learns more information..."

Lilith clearly places the responsibility with Nada. She then informs us that two families seeking girls are ahead of us, but Nada succinctly told us we were her next family awaiting a girl. So we ask, "But if that were the case, why were we asked to travel and meet this potential match before them?"

She incredulously retorts, "We cannot know the motivation of the director."

It now seems the orphanage director is in charge of determining Murre's order placement—but as we learned in Morocco, Rania did not even know about us until we arrived at her office door. But then Lilith admonishes, "Regardless of what Nada shared in context of a Rabat waiting line, you were informed differently by me."

In a single email, she had passed the baton of blame from Nada to Rania and then takes charge herself. It felt like a game filled with continual shifts of authority.

We are also enlightened when Lilith admits that Rania was not welcoming of her during their brief encounter months earlier. Yet she opted to disregard Rania's behavior. Additionally, Lilith only told us about the orphanage in Meknes (the best one of all her programs, she claimed), never revealing there was even the *possibility* of being sent elsewhere. This feels like a bait-and-switch and we were her guinea pigs sent to test the adoptive waters.

We opted to divulge Nada's insistence that she cannot accept dossiers for girls and ask why we hadn't been warned.

She responds, "While she may have stated that she is not accepting future dossiers for girl only, this has not been communicated to Murre…"

Yet Nada had *insisted* she informed Lilith.

We tell Lilith that we selected the Morocco program for the information she had personally delivered: the fantastic orphanage care in Meknes, an availability for the adoption of two babies and both genders, medical exams performed by an American-certified doctor, and the affordable cost. Yet every single factor has been drastically altered.

## SHEER WILLPOWER

She replies that these changes are "true" and falls back on her tired scapegoat of international adoption's transformative nature. "Given your professions, I know that lack of solid and factual information is uncomfortable and you need a more comfortable way of examining decisions and processes."

If not so offensive, it would be the most laughable of all her deflections. Since when does one's occupation dictate the degree of clarification and guidance expected? What type of employment would one need to shrug off these glaring issues and not ask questions?

She closes her reply with delivery of the final blow stating, "All of your concerns and questions are valid…"

**But.**

"I don't feel there is a mutual confidence in our ability to assist you with a successful adoption. I would like to offer an unprecedented refund…"

I hadn't even fathomed this outcome. I am alone when I read her words and my entire body seizes. When I'd awake from a night terror as a child, I often found myself physically paralyzed. This is the first time in my adult life where I experience the same reaction. I am unable to move from my chair or utter a single word. I am swept into a cyclone of shock, confusion, and devastation. She finally validated our concerns, but we had pushed too hard for answers. And we are just one of many families along her conveyer belt.

We were simply *disposed*.

Should we have just trusted Lilith and Nada, despite the conflicting reports? Could we have overlooked some mix-ups? Had we asked too many questions? But where lays the line of personal due diligence and agency accountability? We never asked a question that was without merit, and always maintained respect and integrity with each inquiry.

*Where was theirs?*

Lilith gushed with appreciation for our tips and stated how "proud" she was of us *days earlier*. Now, without warning, we are outright discarded. It is irrational and we wonder how we struck a nerve so deep that it severed our relationship. Should we not have known about Nada seeking to stop Lilith from accepting dossiers for girls? Was Lilith worried we would share this with members of their Morocco program list serve?

Emotionally charged incidents are often viewed through a kaleidoscope of interpretations and responses. When I replay the events in my head, ours is no less complex. I am not a one-dimensional character found in a cheap novel, cut from cardboard, flawless and angelic. My edges are both smooth and serrated, a composite of multifaceted layers and emotional complexity. I am not always liked by others, and sometimes I do not even like myself.

Hindsight is not just twenty-twenty, it's a cancer. I'm punished by this awful, plaguing reminder that I misread and mishandled a situation. I feel like I just allowed a vase of precious value slip through my fingers, exploding into a million shards at my feet. With a piercing shriek, it forces me to recognize my culpability and missteps. But despite my mistakes, we deserved better treatment.

We sent this email because we were desperate for clarifications and reassurance. Instead, we were being shown to the door and directed to count our blessings about this "unprecedented refund."

Lucky *us*.

## SHEER WILLPOWER

The news cut twice as deep as Lilith's email was delivered on the twentieth of April. This was the 39th anniversary of my husband's own adoption.

# Reverberations

*"Life is full of cocoons. We die and are reborn again and again."*
—Sue Monk Kidd

After several emails inquiring about its status, we finally receive a refund check from our former agency. Although we've still sustained a substantial financial loss, we are incredibly relieved to physically have it in our possession. But its finality is damaging. Murre's last email feebly attempts justification with the phrase "since you weren't happy," but the reality is clear: we desired answers and they knee-jerked with swift expulsion. The responsibility for terminating our relationship is solely theirs and we can't even fathom a reason to reply.

Most people would be elated to deposit a ten thousand dollar check into their bank account. But this check represents crushed dreams, and the eight minutes spent waiting in line for an available bank teller is emotionally exasperating. I focus my attention on the muted television airing news coverage, tallying the number of times the anchor expressively raises his eyebrows as his mouth moves. I read the scrolling headlines but cannot consume the content. I shut my eyes and listen to the cadence of soft music playing from invisible speakers. I hear the hum of overhead lights. I try to fixate on the environmental distractions, but all I really keep thinking is, *"Do not cry."*

I am ensnared within a mental fog. My grief recklessly surfaces and attacks like a tsunami, indifferent to the current setting or circumstance. There have been so many unexpected triggers. While many view adoption as a "Plan B," it was always my Plan A. The loss challenges my sense of purpose, hurling me into a tailspin.

When my turn finally arrives, I approach the counter and pass my check to the clerk. An internal voice soothes with the reminder that in a few more minutes I'll be gone. While the teller taps away at his keyboard, I search for a diversion, landing on a plastic display next to where my wallet rests. A stack of lilac-colored brochures expose the words "Babies March of Dimes." I immediately look away, but the word "babies" has already been absorbed like a wet finger to an electrical outlet and the damage floods my body. Though still indoors, I quickly tack sunglasses to my face to hide my eyes. When I accept the receipt, my throat is too tight to audibly muster a "Thank you." By the time I hit the exit, my face is streaked with running tears.

"Failed adoption," the verbiage used to define our experience with Murre. But I find that term too soft, a sugar-coating for what was actually callous abandonment. I also learn that though rarely spoken about, it happens more often than publicized. An adoption attorney informs us that agencies do this on a fairly regular basis, supported by the legal backing of their ironclad contracts.

The repercussions of this failed adoption resound like a wine glass withstanding too high a frequency and my spirit is shattered. I find myself sick with a palpitating sadness while simultaneously warring an invasion of fury. Although concealed in the presence of colleagues, friends, and even family, it wildly ignites when I enter the safe haven of my home.

As it was the center of our universe for the past year, we often shared updates about the status of our adoption with friends and family. When it fell apart, we had the choice of sending a mass email or awaiting individual inquiries. We opted for an email, the quick rip of a bandage. But there were ramifications I hadn't anticipated. Running into a neighbor while at the grocery store or walking to my mailbox set me rabid with anxiety. When our situation is addressed, encouraging words offered with sympathetic expressions seated upon cocked heads, the healing only splinters. Yet when others choose to talk around it, likely to spare feelings or discomfort, I boil with hostility over the lack of acknowledgement. My reactions are illogical and I pity those subjected to interact with such a disillusioned woman. So I decide to shield them from my madness.

An emotional shuttering from the impending storm of inquiries, my home transforms into a suburban fortress. I cocoon myself from the world outside my front door, even waiting for the setting sun to walk my dog, when neighborhood children and their devoted parents move indoors. I am intent on filtering out the noise, both outside the walls of my home and within the static of my own mind.

I don't know how to disentangle my personal identity and adoption. They had become one in the same, and a now part of me is gone. But I retain a pulse and am expected to function like a normal human being, despite feeling so far from it.

Draped in this weighted cloak of isolation, I mourn. And on the bad days, when withdrawing further within myself is warranted, I migrate to my closet. Seated behind its closed door I welcome the darkness and its vacant silence. It is transformed into my refuge.

I eventually realize that a tragedy builds to a crisis if you're unable to derive a lesson from it. This is my opportunity to gain valuable insight desperate for recognition, so I decide to investigate with gentle analysis. And this is what I discover: often, grief fades like a handprint in the sand, eventually washed smooth by the time of passing waters. Sometimes it becomes malleable like dough and can be reshaped into something entirely different. Other times it lingers, stubbornly and deliberately. But perhaps it remains, with its unrelenting grip, until it is truly understood and fully digested. Maybe turning it over in your hands and inspecting it closely allows its eventual release, like a bird freed from its cage.

The ache subsides and clarity illuminates the horizon as I discover an awakening that has reshaped a vital component of my very being, or maybe this death led to its birth: I am resilient. I accept that this is an isolated failure. It does not define me and should not cloud my ultimate goal of motherhood.

We must keep moving forward.

I knew this healing would begin with addressing the contents of a room in my own home that I fervently avoid. Lying within are side-by-side cribs with matching, gender-neutral bedding draped over its railings. Paint chips are taped to a wall and a mural I sketched is exposed in an opened notepad on the dresser. A double jogging stroller sits vacant under a window and gifted clothing, in soft shades of blue and pink, hang in the closet. The room is a haunting reminder and I have not crossed its threshold since our return from Morocco.

But I am now equipped with peace, courage, and a determination to accomplish this crucial first step towards my emotional recovery. I take a deep breath and place my feet on the soft carpet just within the door's frame. Giving myself a moment, I walk further inside, removing paint chips from the wall and tucking them, alongside the sketch, into a dresser drawer. I relocate the stroller to a corner of the basement. And with quiet reverence, I disassemble both cribs.

When my task is complete, I close the door to the nursery with certainty that it will reopen again one day. And something deep within me shifts, finally allowing passage.

**SHE**ER **WILL**POWER

# When One Door Closes

As our lives begin to recalibrate and we settle back into our old routine, my husband receives a voicemail from his father, Albert. His message is brief, but he details a longtime family friend who recently began working with a nonprofit organization responsible for the care of neglected and abused children. Albert had passed along the specifics of our recent adoption failure to her, and though the kids she directly works with aren't available for adoption, he felt she had some "good news" for us.

With guarded optimism, we pull two kitchen chairs close to one another and position Russ's cell phone between us on the table. Russ dials his dad's number and places the call on speaker while we ready ourselves with pen and paper.

Albert delivers a brief history about his relationship of many years with Karolyn and Vincent. He had served in the Navy with Vincent and the two families share a very special commonality: adopted children. Karolyn and Vincent met my husband as a baby, shortly after his adoption.

Upon learning of our situation, Karolyn encouraged Albert to have us contact her directly.

And that was it. We jot down her phone number, thank my father-in-law for his thoughtfulness in reaching out to her on our behalf, and hang up the phone. Russ and I look at one another and simultaneously release deep sighs laced with anticipation and trepidation.

Are we really prepared to jump back into this?

We dial her number.

Karolyn is instantly disarming and exceptionally kind. She asks if Russ remembers her, and mentions having a photo of him holding her infant son. Russ was only eight years old at the time but distinctly recalls that moment because it was the first time he had ever held a baby in his arms.

Mercifully, she doesn't poke our bruises with questions about Morocco. Karolyn understands that we suffered heartbreak and doesn't want to lead us to more, but excitedly tells us about a potential opportunity.

Her son and his wife also dealt with fertility-related difficulties and sought a family through adoption. So Karolyn reached out to a work associate who connected her with Dianne, the director of a boarding house for pregnant girls. The facility was established to educate girls about pregnancy and motherhood, and in some cases, assist them with adoption plans. They were not an adoption agency, but Karolyn felt it was worth having our paperwork presented to them. She made recommendations of what we should provide along with her home address. Karolyn planned to hand-deliver these to Dianne on our behalf.

Although our home study is specific to international adoption from Morocco, she believes it will suffice and suggests we include a copy. She also encourages us to compose a letter to a birth mother including our introduction and desire to adopt.

## SHEER WILLPOWER

Karolyn explains that birth mothers often request in-person interviews with prospective adoptive parents and alerts us to the growing popularity of "open adoptions." Unfamiliar with what this entails, we learn that the birth mother and adoptive parents agree upon the terms of contact. This contact spans the spectrum, from occasional emails with photos, to in-person visits with the child. Although the considerations for our open adoption would remain unknown, Russ and I decide that we are completely amenable to working with this type of arrangement.

We thank Karolyn profusely and with a renewed fire, diligently get started. We decide to work separately on the letter to the birth mother and then compare and contrast. But I find myself sitting before a blinking cursor for too long a time. The significance of this letter overwhelms me with its momentous weight. How do we even begin? What do we say to a woman potentially granting us parenthood for her child? What would she want to know? What would we like to tell her about us? How do we possibly express gratitude for considering us and assure her that we will forever love this child? Although these feelings resonate so deep within my heart down to the tips of my toes, it feels almost impossible to transfer these sentiments to a note.

After hammering out multiple versions with much scrutiny and heavy editing, we develop a cover letter. It could end up never being seen, or the woman who reads our words can drastically alter our future.

Along with the letter and additional documentation Karolyn had suggested, we decide to include a collage of photos. This was something requested for Morocco and we thought it could be a nice addition here as well. Our four-year-old niece flashes a toothy smile as she's hoisted into the air by her Uncle Russ. A tender moment is captured between aunt and niece as I cuddle my brother's infant daughter. There are photos of Russ's parents, my parents, Russ and me together, and our home. Love is alive in every image. We yearn for this birth mother to realize that our family would instantly welcome and fiercely love their baby.

After scrambling to gather all the necessary materials, we mail it for overnight delivery to Karolyn.

It is our packet of paper dreams.

But the dream doesn't end there, because the following night I dream I am pregnant. I can't say it was abnormally vivid or that there were any remarkable components. But however preposterous, a question persists, and its one I find difficult to admit and somewhat embarrassed to confess.

Could this dream possibly be a premonition?

With hands rested on rounded hips, I slowly pace my bedroom, end to end, back and forth. I carry a sizeable mass in my gut and the visibility of my feet is hidden beneath the curve of my belly. I expect my water to break at any moment. Admittedly, I don't even know if this happens in actuality. Do women really anticipate their water breaking? Whether scientifically sound or not, this seemed quite logical in my dream and I retained concentrated attention on this apparent task. There was no air of anxiety, as I felt fully under control and awash in calm.

As dreams typically deliver, the details are obscure, but the emotions elicited are rooted in reality and hard to shake even when conscious. Although never experienced before, I awoke with a richly powerful memory of feeling the baby's weight inside me. Perhaps I'm forgetting the sight of eight tentacles that replaced my legs or Barry Manolo's reflection in the mirror. Nonetheless, a strange (if not cruel) curiosity trails a dream like this. Although it may prompt eye rolls or outright

## SHEER WILLPOWER

pity, I do wonder if someday I'll find myself pacing a room, willing my water to break, and laughing at the memory of this dream.

LAURI M. VELOTTA-RANKIN

# Haunted by a Stroller

Compassionately, my husband, no less painfully afflicted by this loss than me, takes the reins and posts an ad on Craigslist to sell the double stroller. It may sound ridiculous, but this stroller's investigation was as deeply researched as our vehicles. Meticulously selected, it was high-quality with a less offensive price tag than its many competitors. I vividly recall our happy outing to a nearby sporting goods store for its unoccupied test drive. And then a very complex and critical decision was upon us: which color? The gender-neutral orange won the gruesome roulette of choices. It felt the most cheery and reflective of our anticipatory moods. An avid runner, Russ dreamed aloud about his excitement for the day his children could join him during this spiritual ritual. I remember struggling to lift its weight into the back of my SUV, but figured that with the constant cradling of two babies, my arms would grow stronger and I'd soon be performing that task with minimal effort.

The purchase of that stroller served a greater purpose than merely the transportation for two children. It was a tangible verification of their impending arrival.

Russ treads softly, remaining silent about the replies he receives to the ad. One evening, he gently informs me that he's leaving to meet a

## SHEER WILLPOWER

woman at the nearby shopping center. She's interested in purchasing the stroller. I can hardly be privy to this information without developing a burning in my eyes and constriction in my chest. It's a reminder of my unabated sensitivity to the topic and it relentlessly damages my strength's regrowth.

The ghost of this stroller haunts beyond its final sale. One day at work, Russ calls my office from just down the hall. It's early afternoon, around the time productivity starts to fade, and he wants to treat me to a coffee. I gladly accept, springing from my seat and meeting him at the elevator. Together, we stroll to the nearby Starbucks, enjoying a few sacred moments of the weekday sunlight us nine-to-fivers us tend to miss.

We're engaged in conversation at the condiment station, filling our hot beverages with creamer and sugar. Just to my left, the entrance door swings opens. A woman pushing a double stroller glides in and approaches the counter. The stroller is identical to the one we had just sold on Craigslist—except hers is occupied.

We knew we'd see one of its hundreds, thousands, of twins someday, but this was the first, and it struck like a knife's twist my heart.

With ballooning emotions, I intensely focus my attention on preparing the coffee in front of me, hoping Russ didn't catch my quick gaze upon the four-wheeled nightmare. If I meet his eyes I'll undoubtedly cry, so I glue them to the mission before me. I am so weary and frustrated by my quick-triggered emotions.

I tear and dispense each sugar packet individually, adding one more than usual to prolong the moment. I carefully pour the half-and-half into my cup and set it back down on the counter. I plunge the stir stick into the steaming liquid, slowly dragging it counterclockwise. By the time this task is complete, mom and stroller have passed behind us and are safely out of my line of site. My heart silently begs Russ not to utter a word about it or pass a sympathetic look my way. Let's choose to ignore it together, I silently beg.

I'm flooded with relief as he starts speaking about a work-related project. I manage to pose relevant statements and questions. The longer he speaks, the more time I have to relax my mind and settle my heart so it recovers its usual cadence. I feel my internal tension gradually melt.

I always prided myself as being a strong woman, but this venture has left me sorely vulnerable. Anything related to babies or parenthood has become emotional kryptonite.

The stroller is one of many innocent pinpricks. An overheard conversation about an adventurous vacation in Morocco, a neighbor's kind inquiry about how we're coping, a baby announcement received in the mail. And then I travel down the rabbit hole of social media. It seems like I am stumbling across ultrasound photos and pregnancy surprises on a daily basis, from an elementary school classmate, a former coworker, an old neighbor, a current neighbor, my college roommate, and so on. Television provides no escape, as the cycle of life is ubiquitous. Sitcoms excite with unexpected pregnancies, dramas stun with lost pregnancies, and news coverage reveals expectant celebrities and adoptions. I revisit *I Love Lucy* reruns as a safe haven for avoiding the baby hoopla. But I had forgotten about the arrival of "little Ricky" and watch as Lucy discovers that she too is pregnant.

When my mind grows still, I think of Morocco... the trip, the questions, the program ejection. I watch television to numb and distract myself, batting away the thoughts like stinging bees swarming around my head. But just like avoidance, this action only gets you stung. It's

## SHEER WILLPOWER

permitting the stillness that helps the bees pass and you remain intact, free of painful welts.

# A Caveat Gives Pause

I stand at the stovetop preparing dinner when my attention is redirected out the kitchen window to the backyard. Chase races after Russ, practically galloping through the grass, floating over the ground with each stride. I approach the window to get a closer peek and smile as I watch my husband and dog play. When my gaze falls upon our new tree, a veil of shade is cast on both the lawn and my joy.

The maple is still getting acclimated, learning how to firmly root itself into the earth beneath. Too tenuous to stand independently, the tree is supported by a rope stretched to stakes on either side. This adds stability during periods of heavy wind and rain to ensure survival.

We thought this tree would represent the match with one or both of our Moroccan children, but now we're left with this symbol of failure. Russ believes the maple is unhealthy, and I secretly hope it withers and dies so I no longer have this constant reminder planted in our backyard.

The aroma of onions rises from the frying pan and I return to sautéing vegetables and stirring the rice cooking on an adjacent burner. My cell phone rings and I abandon the task in search of it. I manage to answer on the last ring, just before the caller is directed to voice mail. A brief glance at the number indicates it is unknown and out of state.

"Hi, Lauri? This is Dianne—" Now begins a quest, that split-second moment where your mind races to connect the name-to-relationship dots. Old friend? Former coworker? Telemarketer? The sudden association strikes like lightning.

I had never heard her voice before but knew her name and had spent too many moments imagining this call. One unsuspecting day she'd call with words that would change our lives. Dianne is the director of the home for pregnant girls. She must have received our packet from Karolyn.

I can't recall the first words I spoke. I immediately felt thick-tongued, drunk with a cocktail of excitement and fear. I snap out of my mental haze when she is compelled to ask if I am okay. I quickly apologize, stammering through an excuse about cooking dinner and being caught off guard by her call. I twist the knobs on the stove to "Off," grab a notepad and pen, and ensure her that my focus is now entirely on her.

But my eyes frantically scan the yard for Russ, cursing the timing. Realizing I'm unable to get his attention while giving Dianne mine, I concentrate hard on what she's saying, pen at the ready.

Dianne's words are spoken slowly, heavy with southern charm. She informs me that Karolyn had told her the details of our "heartbreaking experience" with the adoption agency and states that she is "more than happy" to help us out.

*More than happy.* What fantastic news! We only knew Dianne by name and had no idea how receptive she'd be to receiving our information, given without solicitation and no doubt, in an atypical manner. Whether our experience with Murre had hardened me or I was thinking more clearly, I worry she may be reaching out to us merely as a professional courtesy to Karolyn. Dianne unnecessarily apologizes for not contacting us sooner, exposing the recent death of her husband and how she is struggling to find her way. Although I could never grasp the loss of a spouse, my very fresh and recent relationship with grief yields a swift kinship with Dianne.

Within the first few moments of our conversation, I know her intentions are legitimate and she's not leading us with a false sense of hope. Dianne is a kind soul, eager to supply valuable help.

I hear Russ return indoors and frantically wave him over to my side. He and Dianne exchange introductions and she shares the home's history, along with a prophetic account.

Their first residents were two young and pregnant girls. Judy was determined to parent the baby while Lisa chose to make an adoption plan for her child. Lisa studied more than thirty profiles in which couples share personal information about their lives with the hopes of finding parenthood through adoption. She was determined to find the perfect fit for this baby. After deciding on a couple, Lisa confided in Dianne that she had already named her unborn baby girl Lauren, and she really hoped they would honor this moniker. Dianne gently informed Lisa that she couldn't guarantee this, but recommended she let the couple know.

The prospective parents were stunned when they learn of Lisa's request, because they had selected the name Lauren for the daughter they expected years prior. But tragically, the baby died during childbirth and the grieving couple impulsively gave her a different name. They quietly decided that if they were fortunate enough to have a successful pregnancy, they would name a daughter Lauren.

And now, when the couple and birth mom get together, they all dote on baby Lauren.

Although the story is not my own, it provides nourishment during a time of starvation, and I am so thankful that she decided to share it.

Dianne informs us that two girls are scheduled to enter the home in the coming weeks. She is unaware of their plans (to parent or find an adoptive family), but had a recommendation for us. The convoluted maze of adoption requires yet another hand off.

Dianne is excited to connect us with Rosalie. Rosalie spearheads an organization that provides profiles of pre-approved families for Dianne's pregnant girls seeking adoption. If we could work with Rosalie and check-off the approval requirements, Dianne will show our profile to the girls if either seeks adoption for their babies. We thank Dianne profusely and say our goodbyes.

Russ and I immediately reach out to Rosalie, encouraged that she can bring us one step closer. Though her organization does not match pregnant women with adoptive-seeking families like an agency, we learn of their many similarities. Rosalie suggests we speak with an adoption attorney and recommends Nathan. They regularly work together and she assures us that he can help facilitate the legal paperwork.

With Nathan's number in hand, we call his office and reach him directly. We introduce ourselves and detail our human chain of contacts, from Karolyn to Dianne to Rosalie to him. We explain that we would like to supply our profile to Rosalie for the young women at Dianne's home who are making adoption plans, and we were told he could expedite the legalese. Speaking with a slow drawl, Nathan is pleasant and jovial, and amenable to work with us. He begins to ask questions related to the process, but the moment we mention residing out of state, we practically hear his pen drop.

Although not explicitly restricted, this particular organization has exclusively worked with in-state families and he warns that we may face some difficulties moving forward.

The familiar sirens of multi-layered complexities blare. And like a cartoon character trying to stop mid-sprint, heels sinking into the ground with a dust cloud ballooning around them, we politely call a timeout. Thanking Nathan for speaking with us, we let him know that we'll mull over the specifics before mailing our first check. But the truth is that we already know our answer. Tired and wary about impending complications, as well as placing our fate in the distanced hands of others, we retreat and agree to reassess—everything.

**SHEER WILLPOWER**

# A Reevaluation

*"Re-examine all that you have been told. Dismiss that which insults your soul."*
—*Walt Whitman*

It's early evening and we've arrived directly from work. Weaving our way through the halls of a nearby community recreational center, we locate the room. Two women stand at the front with their backs to us as they neatly stack pamphlets onto a folding table. We find seats in the second row and unearth our note-taking supplies. The session will start shortly.

We have come to learn about domestic adoption.

The room grows crowded until all chairs are taken and latecomers are left lining walls. One of the facilitators approaches the podium and clears her throat. She introduces herself as Naomi, and immediately plunges into the substantive material as we vigorously scribble notes.

The initial path outlined bears a close resemblance to foreign adoption. The notable difference begins when she states that we are responsible for the development of a photo album. Within its pages, we will include a variety of family photos, a letter for the birth mother, and other accoutrements illustrating who we are, how we live, why we want to have a family, and how we intend to raise our child.

Naomi then points to a stack of albums piled on the table to her left. They're taller than her and all appear thick with detail. My attention is drawn to one embellished with brightly colored, decorative trim spilling from its cellophane-covered pages. I wonder if this was done intentionally to gain attention. Relevant items that can lie flat within its pages are permitted for inclusion, she informs. We are encouraged to tap into our creativity when fashioning our albums, and my mind immediately launches into formulating ideas for its design.

Naomi decides this is the moment to temper emotions, explaining that ours will reside among *hundreds* of albums in the agency's possession. Each birth mother will likely only browse a handful before finding a couple to parent her child. Those who have waited the longest will have their albums placed nearest the pile's top, while newcomers fall to the bottom. She gently warns that it may be a year before our album is even cracked open. This policy is closely aligned with methods employed by international adoption agencies. Clients with seniority have the best placement and are likely to be selected first.

With this revelation, the room is abuzz with whispers and hands rise throughout the crowd. A discussion ensues with participants composing carefully-worded statements and questions about the fairness of this approach. In short, the consensus of prospective adoptive parents is that everyone seeks an equal opportunity to win over a birth mother's heart, and no one wants to be stuck under the weight of all those albums.

But Russ and I aren't evaluating the justice of this process. The metric we're struggling with is the metaphorical height of those stacked albums, not our placement within it. We're presented with a clear delineation of where domestic and foreign adoption wildly diverges: the ratio of child availability to adoptive parents.

## SHEER WILLPOWER

We had contacted more than twenty agencies specializing in foreign adoptions and never once were we informed that there was a shortage of children in orphanages. Rather, the primary culprit for an insufferably long timeframe is the exorbitant volume of paperwork (times two, required for both US and foreign governments) and sometimes corrupt bureaucratic procedures abroad, *not* a lack of orphans.

In contrast, domestically, scales are tipped by the number of couples in search of babies in comparison to the number of pregnant women seeking adoption plans.[*] One resource puts this ratio at thirty-six to one.[†]

Some agencies offer clients tiers of advertising outreach plans, where paying more increases visibility, a theoretical correlation to shorter waits.[‡] So in essence, those able and willing to allocate the largest sums of money to their adoption endeavor "win."

---

[*] "The National Council For Adoption reports a steady decline in the number of babies put up for adoption over the past several decades."
http://www.reuters.com/article/2013/01/15/us-adoption-domestic-waits-idUSBRE90E15Y20130115
"Approximately 1% of pregnant, unmarried women choose adoption."
https://www.adoptioncouncil.org/families/domestic-infant-adoption

[†] This article originates from a pro-life website and is not cited for its representation of my personal beliefs but to support the disproportionate number of couples seeking to adopt per adoptable child.
http://www.lifenews.com/2012/07/09/thirty-six-couples-wait-for-every-one-baby-who-is-adopted/

[‡] The website of a popular domestic adoption agency, *American Adoptions*, details that a $2,000 advertising budget returns an approximate wait of five-plus years for hopeful adoptive parents while a $10,000 budget can result in a birth mother selection in as little as three months. "The more money spent on advertising per adoptive family, the more exposure they will have with prospective birth parents."
https://www.americanadoptions.com/adopt/how_long_is_the_wait

Whether this is the perk of a free and fair market or an ethically questionable tactic, it isn't a road we are willing to travel. And despite our own fertility limitations, we do not want to battle struggling couples. Parenting a child in need of family is our ultimate goal and we are still determined to pursue it.

So we reach another moment of reassessment. We research the adoption of children in foster care who are legally surrendered by their biological families. But we're confronted with teenagers, large siblings groups, and children with severe (and sometimes life-threatening) medical conditions.[§] I view their faces with wet eyes and a heavy heart, and I wish I could be their answer. But I know we are not prepared for this.

We settle in for an emotional spring cleaning and I finally acknowledge our changing priorities. Or perhaps it's merely acceptance that despite all our knocking, no one is answering and it's time to move along to another door. We have reached an adoption stalemate. It's very difficult to surrender something you've claimed as part of your own identity for so long. But by this point, we yearn for a child and I must honestly recognize our shifting focus, as this becomes less about adoption and more about starting a family.

We mutually agree to revisit adoptive options in the future, perhaps even becoming foster parents. But in an effort to move forward, we quietly, temporarily, close the book on adoption.

Running low on alternatives and desperate to hold this process a little closer to us, we decide that we need more control over our future.

Naïvely, we assume in-vitro fertilization (IVF) allows that.

---

[§] Learn more about these children at http://adoptuskids.org/.

## Internal Tinkering

Tentatively advancing towards the edge of the board, we dive straight into an exploration of in-vitro fertilization.

The DC-metro area is riddled with congestion, both four-wheeled and two-legged, but large populations often yield an abundance of options. And fertility treatment centers are no exception as we soon learn about several in the region. After we scrub the internet and engage in chats with former patients, we schedule an appointment with renowned fertility specialist, Dr. Lance Steiger, of DC-Metro Reproductive.

This clinic offers a procedure called Natural Cycle IVF (NC-IVF), a less-invasive and less-costly alternative. Though it sounds like a viable option, I wonder if identifying this treatment with the word "natural" was selected ironically since nothing about it actually is. It may not be as drug-intensive as a regular cycle of IVF, but it is still packed with internal tinkering, needles, prescription drugs, and what they refer to as an "egg-retrieval"—which does not relate to the pastels of Easter in the least.

However, it doesn't require the potent fertility drugs used to stimulate multiple egg production and it is roughly one-third the price of traditional IVF.* Since health insurance lags in providing coverage for IVF, leaving us responsible for its full cost, this seems like a financially prudent decision.†

We are anxious to learn if we're suitable candidates for this type of fertility treatment.

DC-Metro Reproductive is situated along a busy highway in an aged, unremarkable shopping center housing a deli, beauty supply store, and an assortment of miscellaneous small retail businesses. We ascend the elevator to the offices on the second story as butterflies proliferate inside my belly. It's like my gut is attuned to the fact that we're nearing the entrance of a medical office. See, although we're actively investigating this route, I am fiercely and physiologically averse to medical procedures.

While Russ signs us in, I find a seat and scan the waiting room. Baby photos line massive corkboards hanging from the walls, actual proof of their many successes. We point and gush over the saucer-eyed, toothless faces of these little humans and wonder if, someday, we too will add to their photo collection.

Dr. Steiger personally escorts us from the waiting area to his office, a small room with two chairs pressed closely to the front of his desk. He

---

* Some statistics do not include the full set of requirements IVF demands, such as the cost of fertility drugs which can amount to several thousand dollars per treatment. https://www.ihr.com/infertility/ivf/ivf-in-vitro-fertilization-cost.html

† As more attention is brought to infertility, political advocacy gains traction. Although laws are currently evolving, health coverage for infertility treatments has been mandated in only 15 states. http://www.resolve.org/family-building-options/insurance_coverage/state-coverage.html

gives us his full attention without a hint of being rushed or distracted. As he speaks, he leans in, shifting his eyes equally between us. He's verbally direct, but far from abrasive. I don't easily warm to doctors, but I like Dr. Steiger.

Possessing a nondescript appearance, he's likely in his early fifties, of average height and build. His hair and eyes are both dark eyes, his complexion olive. As evident by the multiple rows of plainly framed certificates decorating the wall behind him, he is renowned in his field. Regularly hailed as one of the *Washingtonian Magazine's* best physicians, his delivery illuminates no hubris. He could just as easily be the guy who sells you a loveseat or breezily engages you in a discussion about the weather as he bags groceries.

Upon his request, we expound our medical histories and detail what we're seeking to learn about NC-IVF. He patiently awaits our conclusion before presenting a dissection of each intricate step involved. Dr. Steiger explains the NC-IVF procedure and my very basic, watered-down comprehension of the treatment is this: He will monitor my egg development with regular visits, and just prior to being released from its ovary, a medical retrieval is performed. The acquired egg will then be fertilized with Russ's preserved sperm to create an embryo. If this is achieved, the embryo is then returned to my uterus. Several rounds of testing, in the form of blood withdrawals to monitor pregnancy hormones, will determine our success. There is no sugarcoating in his delivery of the requirements or ease of procedures. He also does not embellish our chances or guarantee its outcome.

The fact that I'm even considering IVF is exemplary of desperation pushing passed mental and physical boundaries because I suffer from one massive, consistent hammering of a phobia: *all things medical*. This unfavorable response may start in my head but it hemorrhages to every corner, tip, and curve of my body. The temperature of my hands rivals that of ice cubes, my breathing labors, and I sweat—profusely. I lose sleep over upcoming appointments for the most benign of doctor visits. I tried combatting this phobia with a shield of altruism when I donated blood, but ended up vomiting into a shallow, bean-shaped tray when my blood-bag was only partially full. (Eventually, I completed the donation, so at least there's that.) And during my first gynecological appointment, I burst into tears as the doctor entered the room. She hadn't even closed the door behind her, and my face was buried in my hands as I sobbed, quaking with fear. So the fact that I am now willingly subjecting myself to such a pronounced form of medical probing is... well, I never would have imagined myself game.

I am thirty-three years old and in good overall health with no pre-existing fertility-related impediments, so Dr. Steiger believes I would be a suitable candidate for the NC-IVF procedure. Unfortunately, our fertility challenges also require my husband to bravely endure a surgical "extraction." Dr. Steiger assures us that the operation is commonplace, and recommends a trusted urologist. If successful, we can immediately begin our first round of IVF.

Russ is just as intent to start a family, so with no reservations, we opt to advance.

**SHEER WILLPOWER**

# A "Crumby" Omen

I plop into a chair adjacent to the hospital's main entrance and unload my backpack. I'm equipped with a collection of calming agents: my laptop, three magazines, and an unfinished knitting project. Russ' surgeon provided a pager that will alert me upon completion, and I turn it over in my hands, carefully examine it. Assuming the indicator light denotes its working condition, I gently set it on the table beside me.

I thumb through a magazine but can't ingest in the content, so I pry open my antiquated computer and begin lightly tapping. My eyes are drawn up, diverted by a woman walking with an unusual gait and slow pace. She cradles a newborn in her arms, the blanket's pale blue trim revealing his gender. The baby is surrounded by an entourage of family. They march in unison and when their gazes connect with one another, smiles spring from the corners of their mouths. I watch them for no longer than a handful of seconds, but in that sliver of time I bear witness to an intimate moment of tremendous magnitude for this family. They depart through a pair of automatic glass doors and in an instant, they're gone.

My cell phone pings with a text notification and my heart skips a beat. My girlfriend reaches out to ask how I'm doing. My fingers are at the ready to reply but I hesitate to respond. How *am* I doing? I swallow hard, entombing the answer.

I am scared. I am scared of Russ undergoing this medical procedure, and I am scared that it won't work. The urologist told us our odds are "fifty-fifty."

It has been a long morning. The construction of an extended metro line, reparations to a major highway, and the usual DC-area rush hour generated the trifecta of a traffic nightmare. That was followed by an hour's wait in the reception area and an additional ninety minutes awaiting Dr. Borman's arrival in a small, windowless hospital room with the heavy scent of antiseptic in the air.

A nurse checks Russ's vitals and begins asking a series of standard pre-surgical questions:

Do you have any allergies?
Are you currently taking any medications?
Have you ever had major surgery?
Do you experience muscle pain?
Do you have any metal in your mouth?
(And so on.)

She continued with instructions:
Take out your contacts.
Remove your undergarments.
Wear this surgical cap.
Climb into bed.
The numbing agent for the IV will feel like a bee sting.
(And so on again.)

Turning her attention to me, she commences with an oral list of post-operative requirements. Caught off guard by my new responsibilities, I rip open my behemoth bag of distractions in search of a pen. She doesn't slow down or pause. I try to absorb her statements about correct dosages and occurrences of pain killers and ice packs and antibiotics, as I clumsily upturn my bag. A ball of yarn unravels as it rolls across the floor, taking my nerves along with it. My search is fruitless and I silently curse myself over packing everything but a writing instrument.

She leaves the room and within two minutes, another nurse appears and asks the same questions as the first. I don't raise an eyebrow to the repetition. In fact, I am grateful for it. We highly value the confirmation of these details as they prepare Russ for surgery. But over the next hour, Russ is asked the same sequence of questions by a third nurse and two anesthesiologists. By the time the third anesthesiologist arrives with identical questions, I begin to examine the room's corners for hidden cameras. Surely we are being punked and not on the brink of an actual surgical procedure.

Careful not to offend anyone involved with Russ' surgery, we courteously explain to this anesthesiologist that he is the *fifth* person to ask these questions in the past hour. He pauses and flips through a folder of papers, but indicates there is no record of the answers, so Russ provides them yet again.

My initial appreciation for the replication quickly mutates into the recognition of disorganization, and my flight instinct roars.

A half hour has passed since the third anesthesiologist left when we're revisited by the first nurse. She informs us that Dr. Borman was caught in traffic so Russ's procedure will begin late.

I try to stop it, persuading with a route of blissful optimism, but my mind wanders and I silently question how a surgeon compensates for a late start. When he arrives, he greets me with a fleeting smile and focuses on my husband. I closely inspect his manner to see if he appears agitated from the traffic or speaks a little too quickly as if rushed. I survey his hands, confirming they aren't shaky from an overload of caffeine. I want to implore him, "*Please*, take your time with this. Please possess the understanding that our fate to have a family lies in your two hands." I want to convey this through some absurd, mystical aura of concern radiating from my very core, but I find myself obediently smiling and nodding along while he outlines the procedure.

Following a kiss and prolonged embrace, I am ushered out of the room as they prepare Russ for surgery. I'm relieved that it's finally underway, but I am frightened. We're told that we'll learn the outcome tomorrow, and undoubtedly, our world will change with this single phone call. I shake off the memory of the last life-changing phone call we received.

I dread the two hours ahead of me as I'll inevitably spend that time wrestling the shadows of "what if's." And now my laptop's battery life is quickly fading with no outlet in sight.

The pager vibrates and alarms simultaneously. Russ is out of surgery. I jump to my feet, hurriedly pack my belongings, and return to the second floor. I excitedly approach the front desk and flash the pager. "I buzzed!" I declare with urgency to an unaffected receptionist. She tells me to wait while she lethargically ascends from her chair and drifts into the bowels of the office. I anxiously scan the waiting room and stop on a man in blue scrubs with a cell phone pressed to his ear. It's Dr. Borman. He sees me and springs from his seat, heading in my direction. My heart pounds. He tells me that he just left a voice message for the doctor who'll be "receiving the specimen." Removing the heavy bag of distractions from my shoulder to place upon his own, he warmly states, "Let's go see him." Dr. Borman gestures to a nurse I haven't yet met and we're now walking three abreast to Russ's post-op room. Providing the positivity I seek, he states that the procedure went well and "the tissue looked healthy."

"Wonderfully!" I reply.

*Wonderfully?*

"Wonderful," I correct myself, embarrassed that this moment has rendered me incapable to both think and speak. He doesn't seem to notice. My nervous chatter flares and I'm now detailing our failed Moroccan adoption.

Adoption sparks a fascinating reaction in people. Most seem to know someone who has adopted with experiences that bookend the spectrum. Dr. Borman was no different and like many, he was ready to share the tale.

Close friends of his adopted a child overseas, though he couldn't recall the specific country. Enduring a long wait, they were thrilled when matched with a healthy baby girl. But they soon learned that she was "deaf, mute, and *highly* autistic." The story abruptly ends there and I don't quite know how to digest its intent, so I simply offer a "Wow."

We enter Russ's room and I'm flooded with relief to see his face. He's pale and woozy, still under the influence of heavy sedation. A machine tracking his vitals hums beside his bed. One hand holds ice to his crotch while the other struggles with a graham cracker. The top of his hospital gown receives its crumbs in a fold. His half-baked countenance is unfamiliar and disconcerting.

Dr. Borman delivers a long list of instructions and departs, but not before reiterating that we should have the results by tomorrow. I take a deep breath at the weight of this single word, "tomorrow."

When he leaves the room, the nurse examines Russ. Her nametag identifies her as Angie, and she speaks for the first time. She's excited to tell me about her own adopted daughter and describes it with contrast and prickled objection to Dr. Borman's story. I learn about Angie's incredibly supportive adoption agency, how quickly she was matched, the ease of their two trips to Russia, and the wonderful blessing of this adopted child. It's a beautiful story and had we not recently experienced a failed adoption, I would show more interest in hearing it. But right now, standing before my drugged husband as he clutches ice to his privates, her story stings, and I just want Angie to leave so I can be with Russ. I want to hold his hand, kiss his forehead, and wipe the crumbs from his hospital gown.

Angie asks Russ about his pain. On a scale of one to ten, he tells her it's a three. She's pleased with his reply, states that he'll be discharged shortly, and exits the room. I visually survey him. He is communicative but his words and movements, even his chewing, occur at half-speed. The muted television has his full attention, so I angle a chair to face him and pull out my knitting.

Several minutes pass when the heart monitor suddenly blinks red and alarms. Russ and I both stare at it, trying to decipher what this means. No one races into the room to address the situation so I peer out into the hall and flag down a nurse. He informs us that Russ's heart has slowed, dropping below 45 beats per minute.

It dances around this number, and then dips again, now at 40. The machine continues to blare. Another nurse enters the room, quizzically bouncing looks between the monitor and my husband. Russ is still heavily sedated and unaffected while I'm so panicked that my breathing no longer feels involuntary and I need to perform this function with great awareness.

## SHEER WILLPOWER

A new device is attached to Russ's finger and after a swarm of medical professionals move around him, one informs us that we need to stay longer than anticipated due to this unusual activity. I am more than happy to oblige so Russ can remain closely monitored.

A few moments after the commotion settles, Russ and I are again alone in his room when he starts to writhe in pain. I track down Angie and she returns with a fresh bag of ice, can of ginger ale, and a Percocet. Soon, Russ's jaw unclenches and his body relaxes.

By 2PM, Russ is released and we're finally headed home. I fill the prescription for his pain killer and help him settle onto the couch for the remainder of the evening.

# Post-Surgery Pandemonium

Today is filled with nervous anticipation. Did the surgery work? Can we move forward with IVF? Will we welcome the weekend in celebration or lick a fresh set of wounds?

I want to stay home with Russ today but his pain is mild and he suggests I don't take any additional vacation days. I am already at a deficit from our two weeks spent in Morocco, so I reluctantly drive to work and regularly check on him by email and phone. We discuss daytime television, a dinner menu, our faithful dog glued to his side, and of course, how he's feeling.

At 10AM, Russ calls. He's in severe pain but can't take another dose of Percocet for an hour. I want to run home but he coaxes me into remaining at work. At 11AM he calls again to inform me he took a pill and has minimal pain. I relax and refocus on work.

It's 2:30PM and we have not received a phone call from the fertility clinic. I can no longer concentrate on my tasks and instead, scour the latest headlines. An interview with Gwyneth Paltrow tops the lifestyle section of a popular website and the journalist references a comment she made years prior: "I am the architect of my own misery." This

## SHEER WILLPOWER

resonates within me and I decide to add it to my list of mantras. It is a crucial reminder during our current state of affairs.

As we anticipate this news, I feel like a passenger on a roller coaster moments before its accelerating descent. I'm seated in the front row, listening to the snap of each tick as the car climbs higher while my gut fills with fear. Will the plummet be sheer joy or utter terror?

Although I don't have the answer, I do know there is no stopping this ride.

I set a mental deadline of 4PM for myself. If we don't learn the lab results by then, I will call.

At 4:02PM, I dial the number of our fertility clinic with nervous fingers. I've been put on hold.

The nurse returns and asks for me to spell my last name. Annunciating slowly and clearly, I'm put back on hold. My office phone indicates the call's duration: five minutes and fourteen seconds. As I await her return, I open the clinic's homepage and images of babies scroll across my screen, one after another. A newborn cradled by his mother... a baby born with a full head of dark hair... twins, one dressed in pink, the other wearing blue.

She pops back on the line and says that she'll need to return my call. But she doesn't.

Chaos disrupts our quiet evening. Russ is writhing in pain despite his recent dose of Percocet. Every few minutes his body seizes, muscles clenched, veins engorged with blood. Something is evidently very wrong.

Using my body as a crutch, Russ hobbles to my car. I quickly and gently secure the seatbelt over him, and with a heavy foot, I speed the entire nine miles to the hospital.

*What the hell is happening?*

Parking my car at the ER's entrance, I run inside and grab a wheelchair to bring back to Russ. He gingerly climbs in and I rush him over to the main desk. I detail his surgery the day prior and his tremendous pain despite the Percocet.

As I speak to the Triage nurse, an opened curtain behind her reveals two nurses playing a video game. Their hands wrapped around controls, thumbs vigorously pulsating. I'm told to take a seat. Nurses emerge and I rise, but they're just passing by, casually strolling through the ER absorbed in a lighthearted conversation.

Twenty minutes have passed and the volume of patients in the emergency room grows. A man had an unexplained seizure while another is experiencing heart pain. A frantic husband bursts through the doors pushing his wife in a wheel chair. They have just been in a car accident and she is pregnant with twins.

It has been an agonizing forty minutes and we're still awaiting a physician. Russ has had numerous bouts of searing pain. And there's nothing I can do to help him but keep a clear head and be his advocate.

A delivery man strolls through the ER's entrance with three steaming pizzas. He approaches the Triage nurse and a swarm of blue scrubs emerge in a frenzy for a slice.

An hour has passed and we're still sitting in the emergency room's waiting area. I plead with the nurse behind the desk but she only tells me he'll be taken back "soon." Russ thrashes in pain while I rub his back, desperate for each episode to pass. In this moment, I am acutely aware of our absolute helplessness. I swallow back tears of fear and anger.

A nurse calls his name and we're finally being escorted past the double doors of the ER. She situates him on a gurney and asks a series of questions about yesterday's surgery and his current level of pain. She tells us a doctor will be in shortly, and I worry about that duration. As she vacates our room, a coworker stops her, stating, "Abortion, room six. Twenty-five years old."

From the time we arrived in the ER, it takes a full ninety minutes before Russ is seen by a doctor.

He is carted away to radiology for a closer examination of his abdomen. While I wait, I dig through my purse in search of a pen and paper to release this anxiety through words, my therapy. The only scrap I find is the ripped half of an envelope scrawled with old notes pertaining to our Moroccan adoption.

I laugh aloud at the irony because I just don't know what else to do.

Russ returns and a diagnosis is revealed. He has blocked bowels. Without divulging the details of my husband's toilet habits, this seems like an odd and unlikely scenario. We're prescribed a flush often given to pre-surgical patients.

As the physician details his findings, he is interrupted by a blaring alarm with a computerized voice announcing, "Code pink." Revealing its meaning, he informs us that a newborn has traveled beyond the sanctioned perimeter, and the baby's ankle censor has tripped the alarm. The alert continuously repeats, abruptly ending with no indication of a resolution aside from its silence.

## LAURI M. VELOTTA-RANKIN

Four hours after our arrival in the emergency room, we head home.

**SHEER WILLPOWER**

# The Gift of Perspective

*"So the darkness shall be the light, and the stillness the dancing."* —T. S. Eliot

I fill Russ's prescription the following morning. He begins guzzling the liquid hell, and with each dose, his pain intensifies. His reactions are analogous to cinematic labor pains, except here, there is no acting.

Russ's threshold for pain is impressive. He not only endures it, he regularly and voluntarily welcomes it. He has competed in Ironman triathlons where an athlete swims more than two miles, bikes over one-hundred miles, and runs a full marathon. Wikipedia refers to it as "...one of the most difficult one-day sporting events in the world."[*] Russ has completed three of these events and plans to continue this practice until his body no longer allows it. Russ typically spends the day after his Ironman shuffling slowly throughout our home due to exacerbated muscles and blistered feet. Mere battle wounds, he embraces the challenge of these physical extremes, managing pain with little to no complaints. And now I bear witness to this strong, disciplined man with an unusually high pain tolerance writhe in unbearable agony.

---

[*] https://en.wikipedia.org/wiki/Ironman_Triathlon

By 3PM that day, I am again recklessly speeding to the hospital, and we are back in the ER.

Thankfully, our admittance is quicker when they learn we were there the previous evening. Russ is seen by a physician within thirty minutes and though no alternative or additional diagnosis is tendered, it is determined that he needs to stay the night.

I remain with him until the evening hours, but they have no spare beds so I return home. I feed and walk Chase but my mind is consumed with worry. I barely sleep that night and press ice cube to my eyes swollen from crying.

Arriving early the following morning, I discover that Russ has a roommate. We never see his face or overhear his ailment, but we are greeted by one of his guests. No older than three, a little boy repeatedly peeks around the curtain to stare at us. Within seconds of each look, he's pulled away by the disembodied arm of an adult.

There is still no news from the fertility clinic.

But what we do receive is a new diagnosis. Russ is suffering with an ileus, a side effect of the surgical anesthesia causing intestinal obstruction. The attending physician tells us that it's quite anomalous for a healthy man of his age to suffer with this, as it typically preys on the elderly. Russ is put on a clear liquid diet and remains off his pain medication to help "awaken" his system. But without it, he struggles to manage his pain from surgery.

The urologist who performed Russ's procedure, Dr. Borman, unexpectedly visits. The hospital's physician had contacted his office and fresh off a surgery at the same hospital, Dr. Borman requested Russ's room number.

He examines Russ's incision, discusses his symptoms, diagnosis, pain, and addresses all questions with patience and kindness. Signifying no rush to leave, he pulls a chair up to Russ's bedside and engages us in casual conversation. He knows that the past few days have been difficult, and I detect that he's working to ease our minds. He doesn't collect a copay or swipe our insurance card. This gesture is simple and perhaps, on its surface, insignificant. But it strikes like a stranger's smile at the precise moment it's most needed, and my heart swells with appreciation.

After Dr. Borman leaves, Russ is wheeled off to radiology. I decide to stretch my legs and stroll the halls of the hospital's second floor. I pass a sign directing visitors to "The Birthing Inn" and the melancholy stirs within me. I urge it to dissipate but can feel it rapidly spreading and I'm on the verge of unadulterated self-pity. But I turn a corner and find myself in the oncology ward. Two nurses move around its reception desk and I overhear their conversation about a female patient struggling with chemotherapy. We're trying to create a life while someone behind one of these closed doors fights to keep hers. I wrap a tight grip around my very fortunate reality.

On my last lap, I pass a man pushing his newborn twins in a double stroller. We make eye contact and I congratulate him. A lump forms in my throat as I speak, but I'm reminded of the gift I just stumbled upon: perspective. And with a deep and revived breath, I reenter Russ's room.

It's a new day and I spend its entirety in the hospital with Russ. He's improving but they want to keep him another night. There's a heightened component to today because it's Father's Day.

I'm back with Russ the following morning and he's been promoted from an exclusively liquid diet to soft food. A small victory but we revel in the good news.

The curtain is drawn, enclosing the bed beside him. The personal items of a male's toiletry bag and wallet reside on the nightstand. The patient with the visiting toddler left two days ago, so it seems Russ has a new roommate.

We learn that he has been admitted because of a spider bite, and that he is (or had previously been), a hospital administrator. We haven't set eyes on his face but his voice is raspy, alluding to an older man. And rivaling the irritability of the fictional Ebenezer Scrooge, he is extremely ornery.

Whether solicited or not, Russ's roommate welcomes the hospital chaplain to his bedside. They speak in hushed voices for several minutes until the patient's hospital phone rings. Russ just had a call providing lunch menu options, so we assume he too is receiving a similar courtesy call from food services. But this new neighbor gruffly barks, "Breakfast was a disaster, so if that's what you're planning for lunch, then don't bother." I audibly gasp in disbelief, partially due to the harshness of these words for the poor recipient, but also because he is still in the presence of the chaplain. Russ and I lock widened eyes, stifling giggles.

Presumably unsatisfied with the answer, he reiterates his point and ends the calls with, "That was a *disaster* this morning, okay?"

The chaplain leaves and the patient switches on his television. A few minutes pass and he indignantly snaps, "Because he's an idiot!" We don't know the cause of this outburst, but we have a visual of his screen and can see that he's watching a broadcast of the local news.

## SHEER WILLPOWER

Adding to his outrageous behavior, he just released an earth-shattering belch. He's cognizant of the fact that another patient resides mere feet away, but no pardon follows.

Russ and I laugh, and this time we're less restrictive with our volume. His ridiculous conduct has me smiling, and I realize that it is my first in several days. We welcome the comic relief this grumpy old man provides.

Around 3PM, a well-dressed representative from food services enters the room. He inquires with our neighbor about his breakfast.

Oh *no!*

I immediately tear open my laptop, prepared for what I'm sure will be an epic answer. And he does not disappoint. A verbatim account follows:

"Eggs were cold and unspeakable. I don't even know what that stuff was for. Toast, it was just beyond anything I've ever tasted. I put it in my mouth and thought, *Jesus,* you've got to be kidding me. The apple sauce was just like eating a [he pauses, searching for a suitable analogy] watery sauce. And that's the best I can say. Now lunch was—fortunately, I have a Thai cook who cooked for me so lunch was just remarkable. I did taste the broccoli soup. You couldn't even call it broccoli soup. Watery flour is more like it. Bottom line: it's institutional food and you're cooking for a large quantity here, but there's no flavor to it. And there was nothing served with it to make it flavorful. And that's about the best I can say."

Our mouths hang open throughout his denigration.

I couldn't even imagine the expression of the poor food services representative but he managed to muster up the following response: "I'll share these comments with the chef to let him know it wasn't the best. I'm sorry you had this. We'll try our best to see what we could do."

The curmudgeon replies, "If I eat tonight, I'll have someone bring me food. But I will say this, I do appreciate you doing this, but I'm just reporting the facts, it's nothing personal. If this were a restaurant, I would not go back."

I consider throwing back the curtain in exasperation and shouting, "But it's *not* a restaurant, this is a *hospital!*" But I refrain.

I can hardly believe the words I'm recording, but admittedly, my disgust is met with slight amusement. I type as fast as my fingers allow, ensuring I capture the whole ugly ordeal. This individual's audacity and sense of entitlement is stunning.

Before the gentleman from food services leaves the room, he peers around the curtain and asks how we're doing. With whispers, we express shock at the tirade he just endured. He acknowledges with a shy smile and a countenance indicative of "Thank you, but I'm okay." Russ and I chat with him for a few moments, shrouding him with kindness to offset his last few minutes.

I wonder if he's planning to stir a dose of revenge into this man's next meal. (And if he does, I hope it's delivered to the correct bed in this room!)

Before the night is over, we hear the old man pick up his phone, dial a number, and bark a request for an iced mocha delivery at 8AM tomorrow morning. He's needlessly hostile. I'm convinced that his silver spoon was inserted into the wrong orifice.

Russ accelerates the sobering truth in a brief but poignant statement: "He should keep it in perspective because at least he can eat solid food." I nod in fierce agreement, remembering the oncology ward a short walk down the hall.

The next morning arrives with wonderful news: Russ can leave the hospital. He slowly lifts himself from bed. He's weak and eight pounds lighter, but his health is on the upswing and I am elated to finally bring him home.

The clouds part further that afternoon when we receive the phone call we've been awaiting since Friday. The surgery worked! We can proceed with IVF.

LAURI M. VELOTTA-RANKIN

# Taking Flight with Clipped Wings

With the success of Russ' surgery and his specimen safely preserved in a medical freezer at the fertility clinic, the baton is handed to me. My first requirement is to undergo a hysterosalpingogram (HSG), and Dr. Steiger candidly alerts me to the fact that most women find it painful. I'm standing at the starting line of IVF and my physician is already using the word "painful." I exhale deeply reminding myself that I can do this.

Two friends have undergone this procedure and both clearly grimace when asked about it. I learn that via the vagina, a tube is inserted into the uterus through which dye is administered and analyzed on x-ray. The overall goal is to determine the health of my uterus, two fallopian tubes, and other internal reproductive plumbing.

Dr. Steiger mentions that he often prescribes patients Valium for the procedure, and before he has the opportunity to ask my preference, I'm a human bobblehead nodding vigorously and affirmatively. *Yes, please.* I may have even handed him the prescription pad on his desk.

I have never taken a sedative before, but if it is warranted for any situation, this is it.

## SHEER WILLPOWER

The HSG test is conducted in the radiology department of our local hospital, the one we seem to be spending considerable time in lately. Russ accompanies me to the appointment and carries the single Valium in its orange container like a sacred relic, aware of my absolute reliance on it. We take adjacent seats in a waiting room with pale blue trim, a watercolor of boat, and a muted television anchored to the wall. I grip both arms of the metal chair with a pair of stark white knuckles.

Russ snaps open a bottled water and places the pill in my palm, which I gladly ingest. He holds my hand while we wait and distracts from the impending exam with talk about upcoming weekend plans. My anxiety runs high and I greedily anticipate the moment that Valium begins to calm me from the inside out.

When my name is called, Russ kisses me and I accompany the nurse to radiology. I'm handed a hospital gown and instructed to remove my clothes. Despite the sedation, my hands tingle, my heart races, and my mouth feels oddly stripped of moisture. I mention this while chatting with the radiologist, and she believes it's the precursor to a panic attack. Searching a nearby drawer, she retrieves a brown paper bag. She suggests I take a series of deep breaths, concentrating on the bag's expansion and contraction. I've only seen this done on television and didn't know that it's actually an effective method to avert hyperventilation. I'm embarrassed to have such a dramatic reaction, especially while sedated.

As expected, the test is no picnic. But it's over. I did it.

I spend the next two days nursing and medicating throbbing cramps, a common aftermath of the HSG. But the results arrive, the feedback is positive, and we're accelerated forward.

Two days later, I'm back in Dr. Steiger's office wearing an oversized paper napkin across my midsection because I'm naked from the waist down. I place my folded jeans on the seat of a spare chair with my underwear tucked inside one of the pant legs. I don't know where else to put them. Absurdly, I'm fixated on this, and wonder if I should equip my purse with a wad of plastic baggies to house my underwear during these appointments.

Splayed on the table like a dissected frog, Dr. Steiger is hidden somewhere south of my knees, tinkering away. My legs are literally vibrating with nerves and I'm forcing each breath in and out. He's performing something called a mock embryo transfer. Unfortunately, no Valium was offered for this.

It was unpleasant but fast. Another item gets checked off the list and we're now one step closer. More green lights illuminate and our confidence grows.

I am directed to begin taking prenatal vitamins and baby aspirin. I'm also handed a pile of prescriptions. I pay close to three hundred dollars in pharmacy bills for an array of drugs: one will thicken my uterine lining and another will help activate ovulation. A single Valium is prescribed for the egg retrieval and an antibiotic closes out the requisite medications. Evidently, this natural cycle still necessitates the assistance of modern medicine.

As instructed, we return to the clinic for a sonogram on the second day of my period. When I envision a sonogram, I picture the scenes from movies where a doctor effortlessly glides a lubricated grocery store scanner over a burgeoning belly. However, Dr. Steiger's sonogram is defined as "transvaginal," where a medical device shaped like a miniature baseball bat travels, well, internally. I hear him refer to it as a "wand" and I wonder if I could "abracadabra" it the hell out of me.

## SHEER WILLPOWER

As uncomfortable as this bat/wand sounds, it's even worse when you are menstruating. Dr. Steiger pivots, rotates, and swings it in a myriad of directions while staring at a small screen displaying its images. *My* images, as he's literally studying my insides.

Sometimes he drives the wand a bit too aggressively and in an effort to cope, I attempt transference by digging a fingernail into the skin of the opposite hand. Perhaps this pain will distract my body from the blows below. (Surprisingly, it does work a bit.)

After several minutes of conducting and reviewing the transvaginal ultrasound, Dr. Steiger says his goodbyes and I'm welcomed by a very kind nurse who sticks me with a needle to draw blood. I'm requested back every two days for additional blood withdrawals and sonograms as they continue to monitor my hormone levels.

During my fourth sonogram, Dr. Steiger has some news to share. I wrestle with the wand's discomfort until he stops its movement, pointing at the monitor to identify several dark masses. What he initially thought was a blood clot is actually a condition called endometriosis. He states that he had previously seen the mass but since I don't experience unusually painful periods, he assumed it was a blood clot that would disappear at a later examination. But unfortunately, that isn't the case. Dr. Steiger explains that the difficulty with endometriosis is that the egg can form behind it, rendering the retrieval improbable. So like a hunt for *Where's Waldo*, we wait to track the development and location of my egg. The endometriosis is present near my left ovary so Dr. Steiger teases, "Spend the next few days leaning to your right!"

We grapple with this new health issue, as it could be a detriment to our finances. The NC-IVF treatment costs are divided into stages so if a round needs to be suspended, patients are only financially responsible for the procedures up to that point. Although a perk, we will have already paid for the majority of the treatment by the time we reach the egg retrieval. If the endometriosis prohibits retrieval, we will have lost several thousand dollars. Additionally, if it happens once, it could happen again. And that doesn't even address the physical and emotional impact of having to start over. It's only a possibility, but if it comes to fruition, it afflicts us with a tough financial setback.

That evening, I scour the internet, inundating myself with information about the symptoms, diagnosis, treatment, and ramifications of endometriosis. Adding not only insult to injury but irony to insult, I learn that women more prone to endometriosis are those who have never given birth. And inevitably, I stumble upon the worst case scenarios commonly found when researching any medical affliction.

I grow woozy from these revelations and opt to abandon the quest. Seeking to calm my mind, I employ a secret sedation of my own as I click on the television.

## "X" Marks the Spot

I return several days later for another round with the invasive wand and vampire nurse. An additional green light brightly flashes when we learn that the egg decided to house itself in my right ovary (with both meanings of "right" being applicable).

They begin monitoring the size of my egg, with the goal of retrieval when it reaches a precise size. This is tricky business, as the window is narrow between the egg's maturity and its release. Once it falls into the fallopian tube, retrieval is impossible.

As it nears the measurement they seek, an area on my upper left butt cheek becomes christened by a Sharpie when a nurse marks it with an "X." We're supplied a pre-packaged syringe and small vial of Human Chorionic Gonadotropin (HCG). Part sci-fi, part illicit activities, Russ is given a brief lesson on the mechanics of injecting a needle into the flesh of my ass. I stuff the needle and drug into a pocket of my purse and we're given strict instructions to administer it at 2AM tomorrow.

Russ gently wakes me early the following morning. Squinting at the clock, I see that it's a few minutes to two. I drag myself from bed and head to the bathroom where he hands me a cube of ice to numb my "X" as the nurse had recommended. He carefully draws liquid from the vial into the syringe and I squeeze my eyes shut. He's not looking forward to this any more than I am, but we've embarked on a mission and this is another box to check. I lean my weight against the bathroom counter and soon feel the needle sink into the muscle of my ass cheek. It's removed with a pinch and Russ pulls me in for a hug, relieved by the conclusion of his task. I press the ice back onto the injection site for several more minutes and we wearily crawl back into bed.

I awake that morning with a knot under the skin of my sore tush. Seated at my desk for the workday, I endure several hours of tilted discomfort.

The following day, we return to Dr. Steiger's office for the egg retrieval. Again, he has benignly prescribed a Valium which I gladly accept. I don't recall very much from this appointment and consider asking for one prior to all future encounters with the wand, needle, and anything remotely resembling the bill of a duck.

Our spirits keep rising as we receive more good news. The retrieval and its external fertilization were successful. We return for its transfer, which I literally watch (along with the doctor seated between my legs) on a black and white screen positioned next to the table. An overwhelming sense of awe overshadows the physical unpleasantness as I watch this speck enter my uterus. This tiny, precious orb shoulders massive hopes.

Russ is permitted back into the room when the procedure ends and the nurse says I can now sit back up. She then vacates the room, leaving Russ and I alone. We are both moved by what could be. We hold hands, talk, and laugh. I begin to cry. I'm not sad, worried, in pain, or upset. I'm just overcome by the weight of these circumstances and its prospects. It all feels so surreal.

## SHEER WILLPOWER

I decide to remain prostrate for a few more minutes, keeping my ankles firmly placed against the base of my butt cheeks. I figure there's no harm in lending this fertilized egg some further assistance.

On our way out of the clinic, we're reminded to return in fourteen days for a blood test to determine pregnancy.

Two weeks later, we're in and out of the clinic for the blood withdrawal within a matter of minutes. We should receive word the following day. With great anticipation, we wait.

The next afternoon, Russ unexpectedly visits my office. He suggests we take a short break and drive to a nearby coffee shop. I'd been avoiding caffeine (preemptively) but I'm happy to join him and welcome some fresh air into my lungs.

We park in an empty space near the entrance door and before I even step onto the curb, Russ is standing before me. His face is lit with emotion as he grabs my hands and hugs me tightly.

"It worked," he says, "Honey, you're *pregnant!*"

Unable to reach me directly, the clinic called Russ's cell phone to pass along the wonderful news. As Russ dances around me, I pause, allowing this spectacular revelation to wash over and through me.

During our lifetimes, there are moments we know will remain with us forever, and this was certainly cementing its place. It felt like we were finally nearing the summit after a difficult trek to parenthood.

And after a reflection of our previous troubles, we could finally throw our arms up in celebration, marveling the milestone.

Just outside the coffee shop's front door, we embrace and absorb the all-encompassing feeling of raw joy.

I'm instructed to return the following week so they can track my pregnancy hormone levels. Russ is called overseas for work, so it's a solo trip when I have my blood drawn at the clinic on a Friday morning. Despite her moniker, the sweet vampire nurse and I have become friendly. She greets me with a warm embrace. "Congratulations!" she squeals. This is the first time I haven't minded her needle and vial.

With Russ out of the country, I decide to invite a good friend over for breakfast the next morning. Ann has been a constant support through the highs and lows. Having ridden the merry-go-round of IVF, she is well-aware of the procedures and has basically kept a copy of my calendar, constantly checking in with me. Upon her arrival, she immediately asks if I've received any updates. Russ and I had decided that we'll tell our family and a handful of close friends aware of our medical appointments. I don't even have to speak the words to Ann and she screams with delight. We hug one another and enjoy a hearty breakfast of bacon, eggs, and pancakes.

My mom digests the pregnancy with more tempered excitement. "It's still so early, Lauri," she cautions. I understand, of course, but the biggest hurdle with IVF is reaching the point of pregnancy. Once the reading is positive, the hard part is over.

Right?

When Ann leaves, I spend the remainder of the afternoon relaxing on the couch while massaging Chase's exposed belly with my feet. Aside from wishing Russ was present, I feel very content.

## SHEER WILLPOWER

Halfway through a movie, I receive a phone call and recognize the number as the fertility clinic. In an instant, alarms siren in my head and my heart pounds as I answer.

They have never called before.

A nurse solemnly informs me that my pregnancy hormone has dropped, indicative of a miscarriage. I'm directed to return in several days for another blood test to ensure there are no complications.

I feel like the wind has been knocked out of me… from impact with a dump truck.

I'm devastated.

We knew getting pregnant through NC-IVF would be challenging, but we didn't anticipate it failing after learning of a pregnancy.

Russ is halfway across the world and I'm heartbroken that I have to relay the news to him over the phone. He tries to comfort me with his words, but I'm temporarily inconsolable. I desperately wish he were home. I calm myself enough to speak audibly and assure him that I'll be okay. We'll get through this, and we'll try again.

We end the call with an exchange of love. And alone, I grieve.

# IVF, Take Two

*"A woman is like a tea bag; you never know how strong it is until it's in hot water."* —Eleanor Roosevelt

A failed adoption in Morocco, complications related to Russ' surgery, and a miscarriage mars both our record and spirit. Though battered, we're still ferociously determined. Dr. Steiger is optimistic, stating that many women don't even attain pregnancy, so having reached that milestone is positive news. I cringe at his cavalier delivery, but digest its rallying intent. We need to take a second shot at this. So with another multi-zeroed check written, I engage an internal autopilot setting and forge ahead with round two of NC-IVF.

My nervous anticipation began with the endless supply of needle pricks and wand explorations, but I've discovered that the emotional pain dampens that of its physical cousin. I offer this hurt to my shadow, behind me, out of sight. My hope is that it dissolves when I head indoors, but it only latches itself closer to me. I am constantly embroiled in a war, imploring calm and peace to prevail.

I've become aware of nuances that had previously floated past me during the first round. The office waiting room accommodates a constant flow of women, all desiring the same outcome. They are focused, mission-oriented, and unflinching warriors. Most are dressed in professional attire, likely taking a short absence from their jobs for a vaguely stated "medical appointment" just like me. They'll slide off their heels, disrobe, and endure the same emotionally and physically invasive procedures. We are sisters united in this fight.

Yet despite this extraordinary commonality, no one dares to make eye contact with another.

Occasionally, while waiting to be called, a woman enters the clinic with a baby. She pushes the chubby-faced toddler in a stroller, smiling warmly at the receptionist as she signs in, and sits with attention squarely placed on her child. And from across the waiting room, I find myself soured by her presence. I wonder if she was once in my shoes, distraught by failed attempts at motherhood. I wonder if she had questioned the sensitivity of bringing a young child to a fertility clinic. And I wonder if those seated around me feel the same disdain I'm ashamed to admit I'm feeling.

I later learn that many fertility clinics institute a no-children policy, and I feel a little less guilt for my thoughts.

The second round proceeds identically to the first, aside from having prior insight into what awaits me. I know what each appointment entails, the ones to simply dread versus those worth losing sleep over. None are pleasant but my sight is firmly affixed to the end game.

It's a Friday morning appointment and we're summoned from the waiting room. A nurse directs me to shed my clothing from the waist down. I'm familiar enough with this drill to wear "easy-offs" like skirts or dresses, elastic-waisted and without the delay posed by a cumbersome belt. And I no longer worry about where to store my underwear.

Sandwiched between a shirt and skirt or between the folds of a dress suffices.

I lie prostrate on the medical table, placing each bare foot in a stirrup as the doctor emerges with his trade tools. The internal sonogram disappears into my crotch and all eyes are turned to the corresponding monitor. The doctor explores the expanse of my vacant uterus and I absorb the wand's movements. As usual, it is highly uncomfortable and several of its maneuvers cause me to wince.

We're told to return tomorrow for more bloodwork and another sonogram for the measurement of my egg. Dr. Steiger speculates that the egg retrieval will happen on Sunday. And as I type these words, a surge of anxiety swells within.

There's no sleeping in or leisure this Saturday morning. We make the thirty mile trek to the clinic. Some days I'm the Rocky Balboa of this process, but today my anxiety seeps out like a sponge unable to retain saturating water. I'm sick of the invasiveness of these procedures and I'm dreading the discomfort... but most of all, I am so very scared that it will result in another failure.

When we arrive, the office is busy. About a dozen couples sit side-by-side in the waiting room. The air feels thick and like a cartoon character, I imagine that my hammering heart is visible through my shirt. My hands are ice cold and damp.

A woman enters the clinic shortly after us, and she's cradling an infant in her arms. I assume she is visiting to introduce her IVF success to the doctor who made it possible. I instantly avert my eyes and try to distract myself.

A nurse calls my name, summoning me to a small room for bloodwork. By this point, the interior of my elbow is a collection of pinpricked, bruised veins. I possess the arms of a heroin addict. I imagine what the world outside this office would conclude from the sight.

I return to the waiting room and sit beside my ever-faithful husband. Russ has been incredibly devoted, encouraging me when I'm fearful and praising my grit after each exam. And when the going gets tough, he becomes my human Kleenex. As tears fill my eyes, his arms immediately pull me in. He's a rock, *my* rock. I squeeze his hand, offer a faint smile, and fix my eyes to the floor. He knows that prolonged eye contact sends a tremor, compromising the structural integrity of the emotional wall I struggle to keep intact.

Although it assumes an ambiguous origin, an optimist once spoke the familiar phrase, "Quitting is not an option." This is typically applied to stories where the vigilant and determined protagonist endures a grueling endeavor only to reach the ultimate triumph. Quitting is not an option for me either, but at the heart of what propels me forward is an innate fear of stopping. I am terrified to even pause for the briefest of moments, because that would likely require a reflection of our situation's reality. And my mind's internal self-preservation apparatus refuses to permit another reevaluation. I am acutely aware of this nearing cliff's edge that overtly reveals our dwindling options, finances, and perseverance. So as I've done time and time again, I convince myself to hold it together a little longer. I put one foot in front of the other. And plan to repeat until victorious.

It's 12:45AM and I'm awoken by my alarm. A glow emits between the bathroom door and its frame, as Russ prepares the syringe on its opposite side. When I enter, he hands me a cube of ice and I lower my underwear to place it on the circle the nurse marked on my butt. (Let's hope a circle brings better luck than an "X.") I hold the ice on site until I'm left with a small nub and toss it into the sink. My husband is wide-eyed and all-business despite having only two hours of sleep. Following the nurse's orders, I point my toes in and lean against the bathroom sink. I feel the needle's sting and within a few seconds, it's over. I find it difficult to catch my breath so I sit on the bathtub's edge placing my head between legs, and I breathe. I just breathe. The pinch of the needle is never as bad as its anticipation.

Russ switches off the bathroom light and we return to a bed that still retains our warmth. We lay in the dark and talk, both admitting that the adrenaline continues to pump through our veins. It takes me at least an hour to fall back asleep. It feels like mere minutes pass before the next alarm blares, and we're off to the races as we make another trip to the clinic. More blood will be drawn and I'll have another ultrasound, via my well-acquainted "frenemy," the wand.

The egg transfer has been scheduled for tomorrow morning. My emotions surge, but not necessarily upward, rather in a haphazard, drunken pattern as I experience the highs and lows of this moment. I've written a few new rules for myself too. This time, I won't daydream about motherhood. This time, I will not look at a calendar to determine a possible birth date. This time, I will not browse websites searching endless lists of baby names. And most imperatively, I won't dare think about how I'll shatter if this round of IVF fails. My focus is merely on tomorrow and nothing but tomorrow.

# Atoning

*"It is impossible to live without failing at something, unless you live so cautiously that you might as well not have lived at all - in which case, you fail by default."*
*–J.K. Rowling*

My parents visited with my four-year-old niece yesterday, and while chasing her around, we passed the uninhabited nursery in our home. I can't decipher if I'm numb, emotionally healed, or merely desensitized to its presence, but it rarely haunts me now. I'd like to believe that I have simply reached a peace treaty with this room. I had even opened the door to vacuum it a few days ago and didn't close it behind me. Perhaps I've been mysteriously gifted with a premonition of some sort of success?

My mom later tells me, "Your Dad's heart broke" when he caught sight of some of the baby-related items that linger in the nursery. She said they were very proud of how we've endured these past two years. It was so complimentary and appreciated, but I found myself riddled with an expanding, hard lump in my throat and fought back tears.

This morning, I awoke with an immediate realization that today is the egg retrieval, and before I can inhale my first deep breath, I'm flooded with anxiety. I practice the various calming techniques I've learned in meditation class, but they're no match for my state of mind. I'm a nervous wreck. Imprisoned by fear, my sanity is being tested and dragged through hell. My silence is enough to clue Russ into my emotional state of frayed nerves.

Before driving to the clinic, he surprises me with breakfast at our favorite coffee shop. As we walk inside, I see the words "Hope is blooming" scrawled across a large, chalkboard wall. I decide to perceive this as a sign, a positive one. But memories of the last procedure cast a shadow of truth. IVF requires an immense investment that far surpasses finances. Hope is the most costly, with the greatest potential for bankruptcy. So today I deliberate: is hope really blooming? I suppose our second attempt is a good indication that we must believe in this mantra.

I walk to the condiment bar to add cream and sugar to my (decaf) coffee when I make a unique and unexpected discovery just past the steel pitcher of half-and-half. A lovely pair dahlia-shaped earrings is punctured through a piece of cardboard with the words "Random Acts of Kindness" stamped across them. A website for a small business is printed on the backside and I'm so touched by the serendipity that I take the earrings and vow to send their creator an email about how beautiful a symbol these blooming ("Hope is blooming!") dahlias are during such a trying time in my life. I want her to know that it truly *is* an act of kindness.*

I decide to remove the earrings from their placeholder and wear them to my procedure.

The egg retrieval and embryo transfer are both successful. We're told to return in a few days to check my HCG level, the pregnancy hormone. If the number resides somewhere north of fifty, I'll be pregnant. I spend the rest of my day trying to focus my attention elsewhere, a near-impossible feat.

The following day, we learn that that my HCG number is 262. I'm *pregnant*.

Every few days I'm expected back at the clinic for HCG level checks via bloodwork. I'm told that the goal is to see this number double and eventually triple.

We spend the next forty-eight hours in tempered but excited delight. My third HCG level yields a 407. It hadn't quite doubled, but we're encouraged by the clinic, as this isn't uncommon.

My following appointment produces a reading of 795. I'm unsure of what to think or how to feel. I'm pregnant, but something's gone awry inside my body, evident by these readings. Knowing the ill effect of stress, I try to calmly plead with my uterus: we need this to work,

---

\* That evening, I enter the website into my browser. I find the jewelry designer's blog and write a message about how much these earrings mean to me. She responds immediately: "I just wanted to thank you so much for writing to me... I am beyond thrilled that you found the earrings... Thank YOU for making MY day - it made my entire evening hearing from you!" She's since closed her business, but I'll never forget the impact those beautiful earrings had on me that day.

we've endured too many blows. This has to be a victory. Please, right the wrong and heal thyself.

But what terrifies me most is enduring another failure. I cannot pull myself up from this again. Thankfully, this fear is so overpowering that my mind won't allow it much attention.

The next reading yields a 1,700. A nurse calls and expresses concerns with the number's sluggish climb. They want me back for a sonogram.

I drag my feet but my perpetually clear-headed husband softly nudges and I concede, scheduling an appointment. Russ joins me. I'm so antsy that I can't even sit in the waiting room. Instead, I stand and pace.

I've deemed the fertility clinic an earthly purgatory. You await the doctor's arrival with sweaty palms and an absence of underwear, and then endure a tense holding of breath until pushing through the exit door. Only then can you unclench your two hands that have mysteriously atrophied into tight fists. This particular experience of waiting for an examination transcends time and patience in a desperate search for serenity. It forces a scrutiny of reflection, a personal tribunal reckoning past choices and an immersion into the abyss of weighted karma. Have I lived the life of quintessential decency or am I too late to make amends with a higher power? I can't help but assess my history of intentional malignancies, whether spoken or enacted. Will the universe seek recalibration and balance with an offer of mercy or one of punishment?

Dr. Steiger enters the room cloaked in his usual demeanor of pleasant calm. He exhibits no urgency or sense of alarm, so I permit my nerves to settle. But as he examines me with the internal sonogram, he's uncharacteristically silent. I don't know how much time passes but it's too long. He's still not speaking, just intently analyzing that damned monitor.

Russ holds my hand during the entire exam, lovingly squeezing it. I begin to cry. In my gut, I know terrible news awaits and I am tormented. I am fixated on Dr. Steiger's mouth, anticipating the words he's preparing to say. He inhales and speaks the words now branded on my heart: "non-viable pregnancy."

Our embryo escaped my uterus and implanted itself in my fallopian tube, otherwise known as an ectopic pregnancy. These afflict a mere one percent of all pregnancies, often targeting women diagnosed with endometriosis. He continues in a gentle tone, explaining that there is no chance this will result in a baby. Instead, I will miscarry within a few days.

The unveiling wrecks me.

As Dr. Steiger continues, my mind permits a merciful escape. I draw within myself, reminiscent of a box television from the early 80s. Occasionally, the scene would become transparent, fading beneath a layer of static. Gray ants dance across the screen, drowning out the audio with a growing buzz. An open-handed thump to the side of the TV reestablishes instant clarity. But I opt against that tap and instead choose to reside hidden beneath the protection of that shadowy veil.

I'm instructed to return two to three days later to ensure my HCG levels are decreasing.

But I refuse.

Over the next several days, I quietly delete multiple voice messages from the clinic. I will not sit in a waiting room filled with baby photos singeing their stares into my heart. I won't subject myself to more poking and prodding to track another miscarriage. I won't even tolerate a discussion on this subject. I am a fragile mess and want nothing more than to forget about this dark tragedy.

But I soon learn I cannot.

Concerned by my inattention, Dr. Steiger calls Russ directly. Learning I haven't yet miscarried, he explains the danger of a "life-threatening" fallopian tube rupture due to a growing embryo. They'll be no letting sleeping dogs lie. An appointment is scheduled and a deep, palpitating dread emerges.

**SHE**er **WILL**power

# Aborting a Dream

We arrive at the clinic on a Sunday afternoon and are surprised to find an empty waiting room. Perhaps Sundays are reserved for time-sensitive appointments like egg retrievals. I learn that Dr. Steiger is off for the day, so instead, we'll be seeing Dr. Terana, the sole female specialist within the practice. An attractive thirty-something with a tender bedside manner, I recently met Dr. Terana, as she performed my previous embryo transfer.

I'm summoned back for a blood test, but it's not with my usual vampire nurse. This one is abnormally quiet and her eyes dance all around me, never settling on mine, speaking nothing more than procedural instructions. Assuming she's been alerted to my status, I can't fault her for feeling uneasy. As she preps my stingy veins, I think about the clinic's practices when dealing with patients who've miscarried or are at the precipice of one, like me. I wonder if they externally label files to indicate those currently enduring these heartbreaks, but I see no outward sign on my folder. No neon-colored sticky note is adhered to its front. Perhaps it's more subtle, like the positioning of a paper clip: if placed along the vertical edge, this patient's been hit with bad news. Avoid eye contact at all costs. Or maybe it's more obscure, denoted by the letter "M" for miscarriage or "E" for ectopic. How many of today's reduced staff know? How many eyes won't meet mine, but settle on my back with sympathy as I walk away?

We're ushered to an examining room and I'm directed to remove my clothing from the waist down, the usual routine. Dr. Terana knocks and enters the room. She's grinning and greets us with a sing-songy, "Hel-loooo."

*Oh my God.* I instantly realize that there is no paper clip, no sticky note, no penned M or E. She is completely unaware of our situation. But how could that be? I burst into tears and she throws a supportive arm around me, stating that all is well and things are "progressing nicely."

She's either confused me with another patient or has not yet viewed my chart to learn of the most recent update. Why wasn't she warned that she was about to enter the room of a very solemn and frightened couple?

I open my mouth to stop her from saying more, but I literally cannot choke out the words. Through gritted teeth, Russ curtly informs her that this is a non-viable pregnancy and she should check my chart. She reacts with confusion and opens the manila folder. As she reads, Dr. Terana's smile fades. She immediately apologizes and buries her face in the thick array of documents. This misstep cuts deeply.

She performs an internal sonogram and is not only alarmed that I still haven't miscarried, but upon inspection, sees that the embryo is growing inside my fallopian tube. She moves with speed and purpose now, and states that she's sending us to the nearest hospital where they'll administer Methotrexate, which she refers to as "an expediter."

Dr. Steiger warned of this drug during the last appointment and I pleaded with the universe that it not be required. If I miscarry naturally, fine. But being a willing recipient of this shot sends my personal code of principles into a massive panic. Both doctors, as well as my husband, repeatedly and gently remind me of the reason: non-viable and life-threatening. There was little rational wiggle room in this argument, but I was so grotesquely conflicted. The question crossed my mind but never my lips, not even as my fingers tap these keys. Am I being prepared to have an abortion?

This ectopic and its newest requirement send me reeling. Everyone reaches a breaking point and I am at its brink. So I engage my ever-reliant, self-preserving auto-pilot setting. It's that big red button under a clear plastic lid that is only to be employed in an emergency and as a last-resort. With absolute certainty, I press it.

We exit the clinic and I cover my swollen, mascara-smeared eyes with sunglasses. It's a beautiful late-summer day. The sky is cloudless and painted a deep majestic blue, and the temperature is unseasonably mild. "I just need a minute," I say to Russ, and he abides. I lean against the car's passenger side door and raise my chin, angling my face skyward. I can see the sun's light through my eyelids as I allow the soft breeze to wash over me, and I feel a baptismal renewal of fortitude. I know external ambient noise is abuzz around me, but behind my closed eyes is a world silenced and still. I identify a transformed mindset and seize it with tremendous gratitude.

Following Dr. Terana's directions, we travel several miles down the road to the nearest hospital. Taking seats in the waiting room, Russ and I hold hands without an exchange of words. What is there to say? Not only are we devastated that our pregnancy didn't hold, now we have to worry about the welfare of my health. So instead, we turn our attention to the television hung from the wall and watch a muted cooking show.

I'm eventually moved to a hospital bed and wheeled down to radiology for an internal sonogram, my second in two hours. I'm returned to a hospital room where Russ awaits me. A doctor arrives to speak with us, and as expected, he joins the consensus.

Yes, this is indeed an ectopic pregnancy.

He details the Methotrexate shot and its "ninety-nine percent effectiveness." I should begin bleeding –miscarrying– with the next few days. I frequently nod as he speaks but I don't believe I open my mouth to speak a single word.

I recall an article I once read about a young cancer survivor who beautifully articulated the imperativeness to avoid the overwhelming and intimidating sum of obstacles ahead. She had recommended looking no further than the one challenge in your immediate path. It's such a simple and obvious concept, but essential for mental survival. I have adopted this approach, coining the term of "bite-sized hurdles." Pairing this experience with our past failures, it's easy to feel a sense of emotional vertigo. But when I blot out everything but this obstacle before me, well, it almost feels possible to focus and conquer.

So I remind myself that after this shot, this one last step, it will be over and I can regain my footing once again. We will reevaluate IVF and in whatever direction we consider right for us, move forward. Again.

A nurse joins our small quarters, stating that she will return shortly to administer the Methotrexate shot. But when reappearing, she is suited in what I can best describe as an ensemble resembling a hazmat suit. She is dressed in head-to-toe thick, rubbery yellow protective-wear. Her appearance makes me recoil, and I audibly gasp. She informs me of the requirement to wear the suit when handling this particular drug. Apparently, the injection that will soon enter my bloodstream, cannot even make contact with her skin.

## SHEER WILLPOWER

As she nears my bicep holding the syringe in her gloved hand, we all hear the disembodied scream of a baby from a nearby room, creating a caricature of an unbelievably distressing experience. I reassure myself that the worst has passed as I feel the pinch of the injection in my arm.

I have to remain at the hospital for several hours, so with Russ's hand in mine, we watch television. I close my eyes when a diaper commercial begins to air and mercifully, fall asleep.

# Stripped of Dignity

*"I had nothing to offer anybody except my own confusion."* —Jack Kerouac

Now I vigilantly await a miscarriage while wrestling a grab bag of emotions. I'm relieved that I've hurdled the shot, but anticipating the dissolution of what would have been a baby is gut-wrenching. Every twinge I feel below the belt sends me sprinting to the bathroom. Am I bleeding? Is this happening now? Yes, this is a non-viable pregnancy but the embryo is still inside and tortures with impossible possibility: what if there's .02% chance that it migrates back to my uterus, unaffected by the Methotrexate? Absurd, but I am unable to fend off this cruel dash of hope. I feel like a ravaged gazelle in the jaws of a lion, violently thrashed around and helpless to do anything but anticipate the inevitable.

I pair the thickest of menstrual pads with black pants for work, day after day, and constantly check the seat when I rise. I cautiously listen to my body as it apparently prepares to rid itself of this "unhealthy pregnancy." I load the car with a pillow, ready to seek refuge in the backseat should the miscarriage begin and bring with it the searing cramps I felt during my previous one.

## SHEER WILLPOWER

Through all of this, I somehow manage to work and contribute to light water cooler conversations about television shows, craft projects, and relationships with coworkers unaware of my plight. Only one person at our workplace has knowledge of our fertility struggles, but he is not exactly a coworker.

I work within an organization that maintains a convoluted, zigzagging hierarchy. Residing on-site with my federal client, I report to a series of bosses within my company (both on-site and remotely) as well as an additional chain of federally-employed supervisors. To paint a more accurate and blunt picture, I inhabit the fattest section of a pyramid: its bottom.

Sitting at its pointy tip is the government's Program Manager, Ziyan. He has recently begun seeking multimedia-related productions, my sole responsibility. It is in this working relationship that we develop an unlikely, unanticipated, and ultimately cherished friendship.

Several months ago, I learn about his family's nonprofit, the Homaira Rahman Foundation (HRF), a charity driven to help quite possibly the most vulnerable children in the world, Afghan orphans.* HRF clothes, feeds, and educates orphaned children, and his family risks their own lives on frequent travel to and from the volatile city of Kabul. At the time, Russ and I were in pursuit of our Moroccan adoption, so sharing this with Ziyan was a natural segue. With piqued interest he explained that he and his wife have started to investigate adoption as well. Curious about our experience and the general process, Russ and I found ourselves seated behind the closed door of Ziyan's office, offering whatever useful knowledge we could pass along. Over time, his inquiries began to dwindle and he soon revealed that his wife was expecting their second child.

---

* Learn more about the Homaira Rahman Foundation's philanthropic work at http://www.hrfcares.org/.

When his daughter was born several weeks ago, Ziyan took a leave of absence. But today, as I glance up from my keyboard, he enters the facility lit with happiness.

I feel the panic surge when I see him walking in my direction because I am in no condition to partake in the dance of congratulatory praise bestowed upon new parents. Yet as if out-of-body, I am formulating relevant questions and smiling along with each given answer. Like any doting parent, he gushes with joy, and the love emits an almost visible aura around him. But I feel crushed under the weight of his sentimental words. There is an undeniable irony because I know that as we chat about his child, I could be miscarrying mine.

Despite the "99% effective" shot I received days ago, I have not miscarried and I'm called back to the clinic. I spend my morning at work, plagued with the stress of this upcoming appointment. Russ approaches my desk, keys in hand, indicating that it's time we leave. I reluctantly lift myself out of the chair, checking it behind me. I am always checking.

Seated in the waiting room of the clinic, my nerves quietly recede and I feel awash with peaceful strength. I close the magazine clenched between my fists (merely serving as a prop) and meditate on this sudden mindset. But within a matter of minutes, the anxiety rapidly surges and despite my best efforts, boils over. I'm now uncontrollably, noiselessly sobbing. A nurse calls me back for blood amid this awful meltdown and I see her face twist with discomfort as she wraps the rubber band above my elbow to plump my vein. I'm embarrassed and angry at my lack of self-control, but I am emotionally worn and threadbare that this unrelentingly nightmare continues.

After being escorted to our usual room, I am directed not to disrobe from the waist down, an abnormal, puzzling request. But I'm content to avoid the wand for a change and where I typically lay, I instead sit upright.

Upon entering our room, Dr. Steiger greets us and immediately pulls me in for a hug. He takes a seat beside me on the examining table. As he speaks to us, his arm remains draped around me.

Some medical professionals exhibit lousy bedside manners, choosing to ignore your tears or pretend they just don't see them. I'd like to think it's not a matter of apathy but rather, an uncertainty of how to react and insecurity in offering comfort. However, the lack of acknowledgement sends one of two messages: your despair isn't severe enough or worthy of the recognition, or they are simply unaffected by the circumstance. Dehumanizing a person during their most vulnerable moment results in bitter, isolating feelings of shame. Yet Dr. Steiger, who undoubtedly meets with distressed patients on a regular basis, takes his time to console us and express sympathy. His gestures are simple, accompanied by reassuring words, but it is the undercurrent of kindness that is most impactful.

He still needs to perform an internal sonogram, so I peel off my underwear and assume the position. It is revealed that the embryo remains lodged inside my fallopian tube and despite the shot I received at the hospital, it has inexplicably continued to grow. We are given a prescription for a more lethal dose of Methotrexate. So leaned against a wall with my underwear now hovering at my ankles, it is injected twice, once in each butt cheek.

I've checked off a plethora of emotions along this journey but a new one surfaces today: humiliation.

Dr. Steiger assures us that this shot will result in a miscarriage. We're given another ninety-nine percent statistic of effectiveness. Exhausted in every feasible way, we don't return to our workplace and instead, head home.

**SHE**ER **WILL**POWER

# And the Silence is Broken

*"The best way out is always through." —Robert Frost*

A strong storm struck the DC-area with a downpour of rain and high winds. Although our maple tree remained rooted to the ground, one of its largest limbs twists a full one hundred and eighty degrees, upturning its leaves. Surprised it didn't snap off entirely, it somehow held onto that branch, but the storm has left it deformed. The next day, Russ stands beneath the tree, trying to assess the situation. Climbing a ladder with a lasso of bungee cord tied to his waist, he cautiously rotates the branch upright, careful not to cause further damage. With the cord, he splints the limb to the branch above it. We laugh at its appearance but I admire Russ's innovative handiwork.

I think about how we too are damaged, but not broken. We're working to heal as well.

Russ has been able to postpone a business trip to Kuwait by a week but our time quickly expires. I assure him I'll be fine and kiss him goodbye when his cab arrives at 4AM Sunday morning.

I spend my day exerting little energy on anything deemed productive, treating myself to sweet indulgences, catching up on a good book, and knitting a winter hat.

That evening, I happily waste hours lounging on the couch watching television. I feel a peace that has been missing for weeks and I bathe in this much-needed tranquility. The only exercise I partake in is a repetitive movement over the fur of sweet and loyal Chase at my side, equally as lazy.

Suddenly, a searing pain fires beneath the skin of my left ovary. I jump up, alarming my dog, and clasp my hands over the spot. I wait, anticipating another jolt, or several, but no more arrive.

It's happening. I'm miscarrying. I'm sure of it.

Spotting no blood, I add a bottle of Advil and an extra pair of pants to the bag I bring to work, and head to bed.

Having to justify the postponement of his travel, Russ alerted his manager to our situation. I understood the need for this disclosure but bemoaned it, and dread knowing how far up the chain of command our very personal news has traveled.

I arrive at work by 6:30AM. Craving routine and normalcy, I find myself happy to be here. I am seated at my desk working on a time-sensitive presentation for Ziyan when I double-over with searing pain. It strikes in the same location as the night before, but this time it persists for a longer duration. When it ends, I remain huddled over my thighs and attempt to make sense of what is happening. While trying to figure out how I can excuse myself for the day, I notice Ziyan walking towards me, stoic-faced. He asks to see me in his office specifying "a new project," and my heart races with fear. Please let this truly be related to a task. I lightly respond, "Sure," as I grab a notepad and pen, and rise to follow him. I'm still unable to decrypt his expression. He steps back and motions for me to enter the room, closing the door behind us.

Ziyan takes a seat at his desk and exhales deeply. His eyes are sorrowful and he speaks softly, in a voice reserved for a friend. My stomach twists because I'm now certain he is about to address this pregnancy. I plead with myself to retain composure, but I crumble when he gently speaks the words, "Lauri, please go home." He expresses his condolences with the offer of support from both he and his wife. I am so appreciative of his compassion. I know that I if I speak my voice will quiver and crack, and I'm already embarrassed enough, so I nod instead. We stand simultaneously, and breaking professional protocol, I hug him.

Although home is a safe haven, reprieve is difficult when sheltered inside. Sixteen young children live in the houses that border our property, and over sixty more reside within a two-block radius. The excited cheers of an informal ball game, the witching hour of an infant's cry, the joyful laughter of merely being together create the daily ambient noise outside these walls. I find myself desperate for the winter months, when these small, vociferous humans are corralled indoors. As time passes and our failures mount, I shamefully grow thick with resentment and often feel both emotional and physical pain when subjected to what we cannot have for ourselves.

With Chase at my side, I fall into bed that Monday night thankful for no additional stabs in my abdomen. But I awake just before midnight in excruciating pain. I urgently outstretch my arm to wake Russ and find no one. I then remember that he is across the world and I am alone. I writhe in bed for a few minutes, desperate to find a position that will ease my suffering. Finding no success, I slide out of bed in the dark with the intention of walking to the bathroom to see if I've finally begun to bleed. But when I stand on my feet, I instantly collapse to the floor. Placing any pressure on my left leg intensifies the severity. So as upright as manageable, I hobble, and I am in agony when my left foot requires even the slightest amount of weight placed upon it. Chase excitedly jumps around me, trying to make sense of what I'm doing.

When I reach the bathroom, I turn on the light and catch a glimpse of my face in the mirror. Wide, panicked eyes and a bewildered expression are reflected back at me, and I hardly recognize my worn visage. I feel equally griped by pain and fear. My movements have been reduced to half-speed but I'm now on the toilet, stunned to discover no blood. This finding jolts with confusion, and hysteria begins to course through my veins. Something is very wrong and I need to dial 9-1-1, but decide to call my husband in Kuwait first.

I haven't yet spoken aloud and when the words escape my mouth, I learn that each syllable results in sharp pain. Russ has difficulty understanding my whispers, but I can hear alarm in his replies. My brother, Mike, lives nearby and is a volunteer emergency medical technician (EMT) so Russ urges me to call him immediately. But Mike is away on a business trip and I am in more pain than I can tolerate. I'm profusely sweating, nauseous, and concerned about passing out, so I hang up with Russ and call the paramedics.

The operator's voice is calm while I explain the ectopic pregnancy, multiple Methotrexate shots, growing embryo, no bleeding, and searing pain. She directs me to unlock the front door for the EMTs and ensure all pets are restrained.

## SHEER WILLPOWER

I glance over at my ninety-pounder, bouncing and hyperventilating around me. I wonder how the hell I am supposed to "restrain" Chase when I can't even stand on my own two feet.

I manage to very gingerly pull myself down the staircase to our main level and crawl to the entryway. I open the front door, allowing Chase to run outside unleashed and urinate on the lawn. Regardless of my pain, my foremost concern is for my dog and giving him an opportunity to relieve himself in case I'm admitted to the hospital. He quickly returns and I lure him to the basement, where he's already well-supplied with food and water. He protests, barking frantically behind its door, but he's safe with everything he needs, and that's the best I can do for him right now.

I crawl back to the front door, yank it wide open, and realize that I've exhausted my strength. Discovering that the most tolerable position is on my hands and knees, I drape myself over the threshold of my home. I remain situated with my front hands flat against the cold stone of our porch while my knees are cushioned inside by our foyer rug. The pain is too severe to adjust my posture. I'm dizzy with panic and disbelief, and the incredible weight of being alone seizes my heart. Never in my life have I felt so scared, hurt, and helpless. Yet this crippling trifecta strikes when I have no one. But as a cold breeze washes across my face, I find something imperceptibly calming in this silent winter's night. It levels the tempest of piqued emotions. I slowly raise my head, close my eyes, and pause to accept this moment.

My eyes then open as the flashing red lights begin to travel up the street.

LAURI M. VELOTTA-RANKIN

# Radiology Rage

*"You gain strength, courage and confidence by every experience in which you really stop to look fear in the face. You are able to say to yourself 'I have lived through this horror. I can take the next thing that comes along.' You must do the thing you think you cannot do."* —Eleanor Roosevelt

Several EMTs emerge from the ambulance and rush over to me, still straddling the doorframe. Two gently help me back into the house and begin asking a series of questions. Remaining on my hands and knees, I answer while watching legs in dark trousers move around me. A blood pressure cuff constricts my bicep. A new set of legs emerge from the hallway closet with a stray pair of sneakers and asks if I'd be comfortable wearing them. I nod yes and he proceeds to lightly place them on my bare feet and tie the laces. I'm equally embarrassed and appreciative, apologizing every time I'm unable to expedite a movement and certain to offer a "thank you" after each task they execute. They work with purpose and efficiency while maintaining incredible compassion, mindful of the person residing at their knees. Someone grabs my purse and cell phone, placing it beside me as I'm loaded onto a stretcher.

They're securing straps across my chest and legs when I catch sight of my next door neighbor, Ben, running up the walkway. His concerned eyes are on me and he's spewing questions: what's happening, are you okay, where is Russ, what can we do to help. Assuming I woke his wife and three young kids, I profusely apologize and assure him (or myself) that I will be fine. I may have further conversed with him but between managing the pain, fear, and activity of those around me, I simply don't recall.

The stretcher is lifted and loaded, and I wince when it hits the ambulance floor. My senses are heightened but I'm disoriented. The blinding interior lights, the swift movements of the technicians encompassing me, the sounds of metal and plastic as they work, and the unfamiliarity of their medical jargon. The sole female EMT asks if she can rifle through my purse in search of a wallet. She needs my driver's license or insurance card, I don't know which but nod in consent. She reads my name aloud, asking to confirm my identity. Before I can reply, one of her coworkers snaps his head towards me, repeating my last name in the form of a question. He asks if I'm related to Mike. He knows my brother, a volunteer EMT with this unit. "Yes," I weakly confirm. He mentions that Mike is off-duty but asks if he should call him for me. Although very thoughtful, I let him know Mike is overseas and thank him. Instead, I provide my parents phone number.

I hate to wake them but with Russ out of the country, I am alone and have no advocate with me should one be needed. I dread their phone ringing in the middle of the night with the voice of a stranger stating that their daughter is being rushed to the emergency room. I am concerned about their racing to the hospital.

Just as we hit a pothole-laden section of road, someone tells me that they are going to start an IV-drip. I nervously nod to convey my understanding. The needle pricks my skin and after fruitlessly digging around, is removed. The EMT tries a second time, unsuccessfully. She sighs in frustration and I hear another EMT coach her on the needle's placement. I yearn for the efficient blood-drawing nurses at my IVF clinic. She seeks a vein for the third time, but to no avail. After the fourth unsuccessful stab to the inside of my elbow, I ask if we can wait until the ambulance stops. I may be prostrate on a gurney, but out the rear windows I've watched the frequency of passing street lights and know we are now near the hospital.

Being transported to the ER via ambulance has its perks, as I do not have to wait with those who have arrived on their own. Instead, I'm immediately wheeled to a room where a nurse helps me change into a gown. A doctor arrives soon after while the nurse successfully sets an IV in my arm and administers a pain killer into the drip. As the pain begins to dull, I could cry in appreciation of this relief.

It's now one in the morning and the doctor tells me he spoke with Dr. Steiger. I'm racked with guilt that Dr. Steiger was awoken in the middle of the night because of me. Russ and I are texting and he tells me that Dr. Steiger called him as well. Throughout my stay at the hospital, the two exchange numerous text messages.

I'm told that another sonogram needs to be performed and I should expect a sonographer to arrive shortly. When she pulls back the curtain to announce her arrival, her belly precedes her. She is swollen with pregnancy. I'm not proud of this, but my immediate reaction is nothing short of disgust. I'm angry that a woman with a baby growing inside of her has to perform this crappy test to analyze the one dying inside of me.

As she transports my gurney through multiple sets of doors, tears begin streaming down my cheeks and pooling into my ears. Her face is no further than two feet above mine but she never looks down. And in retrospect, I can't say that I blame her. But at that moment, I quietly displace my rage onto her.

## SHEER WILLPOWER

Once we arrive in radiology, she wearily details each step of the procedure. She speaks in a monotone voice and looks exhausted. My belly repeatedly convulses with sorrow, and still, she ignores me. I comply with her directions, but do not acknowledge her with words.

When the wand is inside me, its speaker reveals an audible heartbeat. I gasp in horror, and she quickly informs that it's my own heartbeat. I'm sobbing with both anguish and relief, and break my verbal fast with a simple "Thank you."

She wheels me back to my room and as we clear the doorway, I see my parents. Their faces are tight with worry and they both lunge at me with hugs. Even as an adult, there's instant comfort that offers safety and reprieve when in the presence of parents during moments of difficulty. I feel some of the emotional weight lift as it is now shared between the three of us.

My phone lights with an email from my next door neighbors asking if they can help. I reveal the complications of this pregnancy but assure them I'll be okay and that Russ is catching the first flight back to the US. I thank them and apologize for disturbing their family.

We wait over an hour for the ER doctor to review the sonogram results with an obstetrician. They conclude that there is significant concern for rupture, as the embryo remains stuck in my fallopian tube. I'll need surgery. Left with a choice of surgeons, the hospital physician speaks of one who can perform the removal immediately. But Dr. Steiger suggests I meet him at DC-Metro Reproductive in a few hours to discuss a game plan. He recommends a highly qualified colleague of his. Confident that he can call in a favor, he states that this surgeon can perform my surgery later today. Canceling his own appointments, he guarantees his presence during the procedure as well. We trust Dr. Steiger immensely and agree to that scenario. He leaves me with both his cell and home phone numbers.

By the time we leave the ER, it's 4AM. Meeting Dr. Steiger in three hours, my dad drives us back to my house for two hours of sleep. We awake bleary-eyed and are on the road again.

# Preparing for Surgery

*"If you don't know the nature of fear then you can never be fearless."*
—Pema Chödrön

My dad battles morning rush hour to deliver us to DC-Metro Reproductive for our appointment with Dr. Steiger. Traffic is heavy, sprinkled with its fair share of assertive drivers. Responsible for my sleep deprived father battling it, I try to serve as a second pair of eyes, but I'm verbally shooed from backseat driving. In just over an hour, we arrive without incident to an empty parking lot.

Uneasy with the reality of a fertility clinic's functions, my dad chooses to wait in the car. We remind him to lock the doors as he reclines the seat. He nods and pulls a baseball hat over his eyes to catch up on some much-deserved sleep. My mom joins me inside.

A blood withdrawal is deemed unnecessary, but as we're led to an examination room, a nurse tells me that Dr. Steiger will perform a sonogram. I cover myself with a paper robe and strip from the waist down. My mom takes a seat in the chair north of my shoulders as I climb onto the table. Ignoring the stirrups, I opt to keep my legs together until directed otherwise.

I glance up at my mom who has fallen silent, and notice that she's tightly clutching the purse in her lap. Her eyes scan the room, settling upon and uneasily studying the foreign medical equipment pushed to the corners. Almost as if meant for herself, she says, "I couldn't do this," and in words that I never imagined she'd speak to me, she states, "You're my hero."

Even in adulthood, I'm still susceptible to the satisfaction found in parental approval, and something about that remark and the look on her face really strengthen my resolve. Despite the chaos whirling within the confines of my body, externally, I feel safe. My parents are at my side, my husband is on a plane headed home, and I am in the care of a doctor who is laser-focused to end this fiasco. I am scared, certainly, but there's a calming reprieve in the knowledge that while this is actively being addressed, I'm supported within the warm embrace of loved ones.

Dr. Steiger enters the room, greeting me like an old friend. I introduce him to my mom who rises at the introduction. Releasing her grip from the purse, she warmly shakes his one hand with her two, and I know this to be her nonverbal expression of gratitude.

Returning his attention to me, he sighs, dropping his shoulders in defeat. He teases that I'm his "trouble patient" and follows this light ribbing with, "There's one in every crowd." As our polite laughter fades, he prepares the wand and a sobriety descends in the room, a virtual thickening of air. I'm now lying prostrate, unable to see my mom's face, but she's quiet and still. I wonder how she's digesting this peculiar scenario. Dr. Steiger intently studies the screen as he maneuvers the wand inside me. He confirms the embryo's tenacity and takes numerous measurements of its augmented size.

We engage in a chat about the three Methotrexate shots I fruitlessly (pun intended) received. He marvels over the odds of my lack of results and suggests that he should consult me when playing the lottery. His comment is better aligned with the probability of falling piano's target than happily posing with an oversized check. I offer a shrug and half-hearted smile in reply.

The appointment ends with a discussion about the particulars of my impending surgery. The surgeon he had recommended, Dr. Fortis, confirmed the operation, scheduled for noon tomorrow. I'm completely blind to the inner workings of how doctors facilitate these types of agreements. Does one call the other, offer a few verbal bullet points about the patient's condition and oblige after a sort of "you owe me one?" Does his secretary fax over the many pages within my thick medical file prior to the scrub in? Does he inquire about my insurance provider, confirming it's accepted in his plan?

I have performed no background investigation of my own on Dr. Fortis. I haven't had the opportunity to shake his hand, lay eyes upon his face, or make a personal analysis of his bedside manner. I don't know if he's young or old, fresh out of medical school, nearing retirement, or situated somewhere in the middle. Yet I willingly agree to place my life in his hands.

Afterthought casts shadows of disappointment over my inaction. Shouldn't I have properly vetted him? A simple Google search would have unearthed intricacies in the form of abundant reviews, but I neglected to investigate. Did I merely allow others to make life-altering decisions for me because I felt the current was too fast and powerful to manage alone? Did I permit myself to be overcome?

In retrospect, I still find myself unresolved in these answers. But I believe that when plunged into the depths of chaos, we tend to—sometimes, are required to—place our faith in those who spring into action. Had I fallen into the ocean unable to swim, I would have accepted help from the first person to reach me. I wouldn't ask about their swimming credentials. Perhaps I would have pumped the brakes a bit had the suggestion arrived from a doctor with whom I didn't already have a relationship. I was fortunate that my rescuer was a proficient and fast swimmer, armed with a life preserver.

Before my mom and I depart, Dr. Steiger puts his hand on my shoulder and reassuringly reminds me that he will be present for tomorrow's surgery. I place my hand atop his and squeeze.

**SHE**ER **WILL**POWER

## Surgery Imminent

Dr. Steiger sends me home with instructions to begin a bowel prep. He states that it's a common pre-surgical practice and would like me to complete it for tomorrow's procedure. A nurse recommends I purchase a container of baby wipes, assuring me that I'll have a very sore tush once the "cleanse" is complete. Considering the objective of my surgery, there's a twisted irony in buying wipes meant for babies. I don't truly register her ominous warning, but I do make the purchase. (This serves me well, and if undergoing a similar requirement, I strongly recommend the benevolence of these wipes to toilet paper.)

Unfamiliar with the particulars, I'm relieved to know that my job is to simply drink lime-flavored fluid. Sounding vastly better than needles and internal sonograms, I don't complain.

The prep disguises itself in two pretty, petite glass bottles, and I contemplate saving one for a single flower to place on my kitchen's windowsill. At ten-ounces each, just larger than a can of soda, I ingest the first stopping twice for breaths of air. It's not Kool Aid, but it isn't bad.

I plant myself on the couch but before I can engross myself in the plot of a movie, I hit pause on the remote and race to the bathroom.

Sparing the specifics, it's unpleasant. The next few hours proceed like coping with a fierce stomach bug that only exits from the bottom. Now my belly is out of sorts, and with a diet restricted to liquids, I can't tame it with crackers or a banana.

Four hours after I've emptied the first bottle, my mom approaches with the second, and my stomach lurches at its sight. "I just need a minute," I warn her, placing a hand over my mouth and retreating a step. She offers a slew of encouragement and though my head is in the game, my stomach calls another timeout. I raise the bottle to my lips and withdraw it immediately. "Oh no," I tell her with concern, "I won't be able to keep this down." She suggests we begin with a spoonful of the sanctioned blue gelatin and then take a sip. I oblige but it sloshes around my insides and I'm literally sweating as I work to contain it. I need to sit. I convince myself that somehow, in some way, standing is compounding the problem and sitting will reduce the nausea. I can't bring the bottle to my lips, so I find a shot glass and fill it. But my college days are too far in my rearview and I'm unable to guzzle it. Instead, I opt to nurse. Slow and steady wins the race, right? Gravity forces it down but I'm doing battle to keep it there.

I close my eyes, take a few deep breaths, and soldier on. More of the gelatinous blue substance and another ounce of carbonated hell run down my throat.

But then it happens.

I catapult from my seat and sprint to the bathroom. I'm just in time to furiously vomit liquid, tinting the toilet water a shade of brilliant blue.

I persuade myself that postponing an hour may generate a more productive outcome, so I coat my belly with the blue gelatin and try again.

## SHEER WILLPOWER

The result is the same. I'm the vulgar mutation of an outdoor fountain where water escapes the puckered lips of a cherub into the vessel below.

What is it they say about insanity, the repeated duplication of efforts met with unchanged results? I'm a fast learner and easily concede defeat to the fizzy lime-flavored liquid. I resolutely pour the remainder of the solution down the bathroom sink. A devil in disguise and undeserving of a flower, I toss the glass into the recycling bin.

I awake early the following morning and linger in the shower. I don't know how soon I'll be able to bathe again so I scrub with vigor. I wonder what it's like to clean around an incision, how it should be managed, how delicately to treat it, how long it will take to fully heal. Will I be defaced with a scar, the continual reminder of a pregnancy gone awry? I step out of the shower just in time to hear Chase's nails scamper across the floor as he barks at the front door. Familiar with the pitch of his yelps, I quickly throw on a bathrobe and run downstairs. I know relief has arrived as I hear the metal of a key searching the lock for entrance. The door opens and there is Russ, home after a long flight from Kuwait. Dragging his luggage behind him, he drops it and advances towards me. Engulfing me in a lasting hug, I forget about my troubles and bask in the joy of having him home. With Russ at my side, I am safe.

My mom sits with me in the hospital waiting room while Russ parks the car. She remains positive and distracts me with a myriad of topics, none relating to my surgery or babies. I may have drifted during the conversation, but just hearing her voice, calm and steady, keeps my emotions in check.

I sit upon a balanced scale of fear and relief. The knowledge that an end is in sight provides a sense of overdue liberation. These recent weeks of hardship will soon be in my past, serving as nothing more than a crappy memory. I've been living in a suspended state of animation and am eager to resume life's under-appreciated normalcy.

But I am quite terrified. In my early twenties, I had my four wisdom teeth simultaneously pulled with the assistance of twilight sedation. This was the closest contender I've had to actual surgery. So my expectations are as vivid as my imagination, spanning all corners of crazy. Russ suffered an awful side effect to anesthesia. What if I react similarly? And what of my recovery, will I bounce back or will this take a significant amount of time? How will I cope with the pain?

I also still bear the tremendous weight of its ethical implications. When the dust settles, will I be haunted by my actions?

Russ joins me as I'm ushered back to another waiting area, the room delineated by a curtain. The chain of plastic clips strike one another in succession as they're suddenly pulled back with force, revealing Dr. Steiger. He's dressed in powder blue scrubs and jokes about the comfort compared to his daily office attire of a shirt and tie. He runs through a series of medical questions, and I realize it's my time for confession. I sheepishly admit that I did not drink the second bottle required for the bowel prep. Before he can reply, I speak rapidly, detailing a gallant effort but, oh, the vomit. Reacting with indifference, he shrugs it off. He nonchalantly states that it wasn't even really necessary.

Had I not needed him in that moment, my hands might have been wrapped around his neck.

"My wife asked how that poor lady is doing," he tells us. I can't stifle a laugh. You know you're in bad shape when one of the most sought after fertility doctors finds your tale so pathetic that he recounts it to his wife.

## SHEER WILLPOWER

We learn that surgery has been postponed half an hour. I'm permitted one visitor at a time in the pre-surgical room, so Russ and my mom take turns sitting by my bedside. A nurse named Helen introduces herself and asks my mom for a few minutes of privacy. Helen is simply delightful. She hands me a gown as well as a bag for my clothing, chatting all the while. Aware of the reason for my surgery, she offers encouragement. She tells me that we'll be able to try again in three months. She supplies me with the sage advice of researching homeopathic routes. On a packet of a medical wipes, she scribbles down the name of a book about natural remedies to promote pregnancy. It is authored by a renowned doctor, she reassures. Assuming she doesn't know we're IVF patients, I enjoy her gentle and upbeat demeanor, so I stay mum on the particulars. She begins an IV drip, and I believe it is the ninth time in the last four days that my arm greets a needle.

Russ returns to keep me company, but his visit is temporary. Dr. Steiger appears and states that they're ready to begin. My heart races and as hard as I try to fight it, I silently cry while hugging Russ good-bye. I seize his arm tightly but my constricted throat won't permit the words to escape. We lock eyes and in that moment, my emotions subside because I realize he knows what I'm unable to articulate. I loosen my grip as they wheel me away.

Dr. Steiger and I arrive in the operating room where several scrub-suited individuals scurry around as they make preparations. The room is larger than I had expected with walls lined in pale green tiles, reminiscent of public restrooms. Large, metal-based lights are wheeled towards me and placed around my bed. As they are switched on, the ambient noise begins to mute and my mind's precariously stacked pile of fear and dark thoughts mercifully fade to black.

LAURI M. VELOTTA-RANKIN

## An Entangled Juxtaposition

As I awake from surgery, I find myself laying on a gurney, covered with a sheet neatly folded just above my waist. Blurry fluorescent lights illuminate overhead and the cadence of muffled chatter surrounds me. A foreign, sluggish sensation courses through my body. My mind is thick, muddled with sedation. I believe I am situated along a hospital corridor, but in retrospect, that seems unlikely.

The sound of crying babies fill my ears, or perhaps it is just one. I'm unable to make the distinction. I'm in such a fog, identifying and processing the sound, but unable to relate it to my situation. The face of an older nurse suddenly appears over my hospital bed. I do not recognize her, but she seems to know me. "Lauri, honey," she gently states, "I'm going to move your bed so you don't have to hear that. I'm so sorry." My comprehension hangs on the cusp of consciousness as the sweet nurse apologizes. And like defibrillator paddles returning a body to life, I'm jolted back, instantly remembering where I am and why. Her sensitivity, seeking to distance me from a baby's cry, brings about an escalating sound and I soon realize it's my own voice. I'm crying. I'm more affected by her consideration than the correlation to a wailing child. She kindly places a wad of tissues in my palm, enclosing my fingers around them. Tenderly patting my hand, she turns and vanishes. And as tears fill my ears, I drift back into the tranquil abyss of unconsciousness.

I never see the face or shake the hand of Dr. Fortis, the surgeon who removed my ectopic pregnancy. Instead, Doctor Steiger provides a comprehensive post-op report. He informs us that the embryo stretched my fallopian tube beyond repair requiring its removal. With this serving as one of only two paths for an egg's travel, my chance of becoming pregnant in the future is substantially reduced. And it's compounded by the recent diagnosis of endometriosis, which Dr. Steiger had planned to remove while my insides were exposed. But more pervasive than expected, they left it untouched, stating that it would require a separate surgery.

The following morning I awake to find myself in the comfort of my own bed, unable to recall how I got there. I rise slowly, straining to sit upright. And in an instant, as quick as the sharp snap of finger against thumb, my memory surges. As my eyes begin to focus, so does my reality of what transpired the day before.

The midsection of my body aches like it's recovering from a workout of a thousand sit-ups. The surgery warranted three small incisions: one over each ovary, just north of the elastic band on a pair of low-rise underwear, and the third sits just beneath my belly button. They remain covered by bandages but my midsection balloons outward, swollen with the aftermath of an operation. Examining my profile in the mirror, I wonder if this is what I would look like during the early stages of pregnancy.

A staircase consisting of sixteen steps separate the second floor from the main level in my home. I descend the first few without significant difficulty, but by the fifth step, my abdomen is ablaze with excruciating pain. I take a few additional steps down and soon realize that I'm in trouble. Halfway between floors I've become immobile, incapable of moving up or down. Russ bolts up the stairs and asks what he can do to help, but I have nothing to offer. He suggests carrying me the rest of the way, but fearing the possibility of added pain or a fall, I decline. Instead, I lean on him for support as I take each step. By the time we reach the bottom of the stairs, I'm sweating and experiencing pain that rivals the night I called for an ambulance. Feeling both faint and nauseous, I drape myself over the bannister for several minutes.

When I remove the bandages, I am taken aback by the incisions. My body is left with three scars, each the size of pennies and bearing the resemblance of an "X". I pondered the symbolism of three strikes: Morocco, IVF (round 1), IVF (round 2). I feel a strange juxtaposition of pity and pride. My heart broke three distinct times during these attempts to call a child my own, yet I welcome their tattooed memories on my body.*

Dr. Steiger calls to inquire about my recovery. He said that I should fully recuperate in about one week. But it's close to three weeks before I can ride comfortably in a car again. I mention this during a follow-up appointment and he tells me this is likely due to my small frame and Dr. Fortis' "big hands" working under my skin. Russ perceives this explanation as a joke, and perhaps it was, but I'm not as convinced. Either way, I cringe every time I think about it.

Despite the pain, I spend my first few post-op days in a state of drug-induced appreciation laced with unadulterated relief. Fearing for my life, I'm now free of danger and immensely grateful for good health. This mysterious calm after an influx of grief is so tremendous, I feel

---

* While the middle incision eventually blends into the wrinkles of my belly button, the other two remain visible five years later (both retaining their x-shapes). And I still preserve this sacred mindset about them. A part of me, they deserve their place.

## SHEER WILLPOWER

more closely attuned to my spirit. Mystically spectacular, the thick, heavy, often impermeable soul's door opens when at your lowest. During those profoundly difficult moments of life, its presence is revealed through a brief peek, as if a finger had been permitted to graze it. And with it came rejuvenation and the ability to stand once again.

We are showered in kindness, receiving thoughtful emails and cards, and accepting deliveries of flowers and fruit baskets. Weakened by a compilation of disappointments, my hope begins to restore itself through an outpouring of love from those closest to us.

Sometimes though, my gratitude is disrupted by unfortunate stumbles, thrusting me right back into the dark hole of grief. One weekday, shortly following surgery, I slowly wobble to answer a rung doorbell. I arrive as the delivery man is climbing back into his truck. We exchange waves and he drives away. The package he left is large and as I carefully bend down to read the label, I smile, believing we're being gifted by another kind friend or family member. But like a fuzzy image coming into focus, I read the small packaging label indicating that it's a case of baby formula. Expecting her fourth child, it belongs to my next door neighbor.

Several days later, I'm alerted to a questionable charge on my credit card. I log into my account and locate a purchase made in New Jersey—from the retailer *buybuy BABY*.

We're not spared when checking the mail, as we become unwitting recipients of our local hospital's outreach efforts. Letters with the words "The Birthing Inn" are stamped across the envelope. They are immediately disposed.

Often, I could shake free of these gloomy reminders, but sometimes my resilience takes longer to regain its shape and these impressions stick to me like motor oil.

Additionally, I grow exhausted of the lingering pain from surgery. A sneeze once resulted in pain so intense, I braced myself to the back of a kitchen chair to keep from falling. Once I regained composure, I threw my shirt up to examine the stitches, sure that I had burst through each one.

But I sail through many days without elevated negativity regarding our situation. Grief is minimized by no longer being the receptacle of a dangerous health condition. The past few weeks involved mourning this loss and now my attention is redirected to recovery for all planes of my being: mind, body, and soul. The difficult weeks dissipate into days, then into single moments. Its presence remains and certainly will never be forgotten, but is accepted as a segment of my history—one I'm starting to make peace with.

Running low on vacation days (quite the vacation!) but still unable to ride in a car without considerable pain, Ziyan informs my supervisor that he has provided me work to do from home, unprecedented for our contract. I'm greatly relieved that I won't be subjected to the forty-minute commute, and I'm also reminded of my good fortune. I really couldn't have asked for a kinder boss (in reality, a boss several levels above my actual boss) during this tumultuous time in my life.

When I finally return to work the following week, I am thankful to have Russ at the wheel, as he transports us both to and from the office. He drives while I concentrate on road conditions, seeking out the dreaded potholes. Russ tries to safely maneuver around them but when unavoidable, I lift my tush from the passenger seat and hover above it so my abdomen doesn't absorb the shock. I frequently arrive in the office with a pair of sore arms from the repetition of this movement. But returning to my usual routine was beautifully reviving.

Dr. Steiger reaffirms what Helen had told me prior to surgery: we cannot revisit IVF for another three months due to the lingering effects of Methotrexate. It poses too much of a fetal health risk should a pregnancy arise. But even without this mandatory deferment, I'm uncertain I want to battle the physical and emotional demands a third time. Reality pays a visit: I'm down one of two fallopian tubes, my endometriosis is rife with complications, and the increased risk of an ectopic reoccurrence is now one in ten.[†]

The late Maya Angelou had once brilliantly stated, "The horizon leans forward, offering you space to place new steps of change." And as my horizon shifts, I too lean forward in search of redirection.

---

[†] http://www.webpages.uidaho.edu/ngier/ectopicagain.htm

LAURI M. VELOTTA-RANKIN

# When Stories are Shared

*"We cultivate love when we allow our most vulnerable and powerful selves to be deeply seen and known..."* —Brené Brown

Peering through the blinds from the bedroom window, I look down on the backyard to examine our maple tree. It has required the support of stakes to remain safely rooted in the earth, but if left in place too long, the ropes will constrict the trunk of the burgeoning tree, slicing into its flesh. This damage invites pests and disease, both critical threats to its fundamental survival. The time has arrived to release the scaffolding and grant its freedom.

I think about my own liberation and its unexpected influence. In the past, I would crumble with shameful ease under the weight of adversity. So to pursue this goal with such obstinate persistence has been wildly uncharacteristic. I have *never* been this tough, never so tenacious.

And yet, haven't I just proven that I am? Like the maple, I too can survive untethered.

When planning to adopt from Morocco, we shared our news like conventional, expectant parents. I was happy to oblige, at length, when asked for updates. Excited and fulfilled, I withheld few details aside from the mounting financial costs.

After it fell apart and we finally decided to embark on our next family-growing venture, this new dealing of cards was held closer to our chests. I divulged little, rarely speaking of the exploration of other options. We directly identified with the idiom "once bitten, twice shy." Composing an email to family and friends about our failed adoption forced pressure upon a bruise. It was painful to recount the story and quite frankly, embarrassing as well. I wondered if it was a misstep equivalent to revealing a pregnancy before the medically recommended timeframe.

I am reminded of a fateful childhood dance class. Not an exceedingly talented student, I was more interested in conversing with my good friend, Linda. After several unheeded warnings to stop talking, the dance instructor, Miss Erica, took action. Mid-routine, she stopped the cassette and marched out of the studio without speaking a word. A hush fell over the room as we cast quizzical looks at one another. A cluster of young girls, we stood awkwardly in our black leotards and tight buns, waiting for a conclusion to Miss Erica's sudden absence. A few moments later, she returned with a roll of industrial tape in hand. With a smug smile, she advanced toward Linda and me, and proceeded to seal both our mouths shut with several pieces of tape. I vividly recall the sound of each ribbon being pulled and sliced. Although old enough to recognize our disobedience, we were still single-digits in age. Something that would have likely gotten Miss Erica fired today, instilled fear and respect from our group in the mid-eighties. Linda defiantly ripped the tape from her mouth, but shrouded in shame, mine remained intact.

Implementing Miss Erica's silencing method, we had figuratively sealed our mouths. Russ and I decided that our IVF voyage should be more aligned with tradition: it would stay our private business until we reach pregnancy and are prepared to share the news.

But as we slid down the bannister of IVF, the bumps we sustained along the way became increasingly difficult to conceal. And so I reversed course entirely, proactively choosing not to remain locked inside myself, and began to share freely. When asked if we would try adoption again, I'd say that we tried IVF twice. If that news didn't trigger a contorted grimace from the inquirer, I'd divulge that we suffered a miscarriage the first try, and the second resulted in an ectopic pregnancy. I don't know what I expected from imparting such deeply personal information, but most reactions took me by surprise. I not only received support, but many revealed struggles of their own.

A neighborhood block party was met with perfect weather, festive moods, and a cornucopia of food. Yet I bore a tremendous pit in my stomach and hole in my heart. Clustered with the masses, I was occupied in light conversation when a stray ball entered my peripheral. I walked several feet outside the group's perimeter to return it to the kids playing up the street when a neighbor approached me. She's someone I know those general details about: business professional turned stay-at-home mom, always very upbeat and pleasant-natured. Our conversation leads me to reveal our first miscarriage. I discovered that she too had spent several years engaged in a fertility battle. And during it, she suffered two miscarriages. She offers comfort, support, and the most appreciated sentiment, hope.

Another unexpected conversation occurred during an early evening walk with Chase. A neighbor, supervising her young child riding his bicycle, stopped me to express her condolences about Morocco. Her tone, mannerism, and expression projected more than a quick, obligatory courtesy. She looked at me deeply, kindly. I stood before her contemplating the choice of exclusively offering gratitude, or submitting more of myself and my story. I opted for the latter, and told her that I had surgery for an ectopic pregnancy just a few weeks prior. She confided that she knew the pain all too well, as she too had suffered the same fate. She didn't tell me this dismissively or as a pep talk, as if that was a rite of passage before a healthy pregnancy. She spoke of the same inner turmoil and grief. She understood it and she understood me. I was eternally grateful that barely friends, she shared such an intimate part of her personal history.

And it was with these and several other moments that I haphazardly stumble upon an invaluable lesson. When we communicate our hardships, as the wall of ego falls and vulnerability is at its peak, people often receive with an equal measurement of their own exposure. Not only was I surprised by those who had traveled similar paths, but I gained insight from the revelation of each experience. I discovered that I had thought, uttered, written their same words of suffering. I also learned about their individual perspectives. For instance, while one woman sought comfort in God's will, the other squarely pointed a finger at faulty biology. Coping methods were proposed, as were the instances of acceptance and outcomes of peace.

Above all, I finally realized that I'm not chained to strife, and telling my story releases me from the colossal weight of self-imposed captivity.

# A Second Look

*"If you can't fly then run. If you can't run then walk. If you can't walk then crawl. But whatever you do you have to keep moving forward."* —Dr. Martin Luther King, Jr.

After our Moroccan adoption imploded, we had explored domestic adoption. But with it, we had a complicated relationship, and had crossed it off our list for a variety of reasons.

First and foremost, we felt morally conflicted when learning about the disproportionate ratio of available babies to prospective adoptive parents. As noted earlier in this book, one resource stated that for every one child, there were *thirty-six* waiting couples. We wanted a child who needed a home—we didn't want to be a home that needed a child.

Additionally, foreign adoption presents children who have been legally severed from their biological parents, while domestic adoption resides at the polar opposite end of this spectrum. Domestic agencies work almost entirely with pregnant women seeking adoption plans. But as an agency representative had informed us, of every five women seeking to relinquish her unborn child, one inevitably changes her mind. This change of heart could occur while pregnant, immediately after birth, or while the baby is in the temporary custody of adoptive parents. (Once a baby is born and the biological mother signs the adoption paperwork permitting the adoption of her biological child, she has a pre-established number of days to reverse her decision; this amount of time differs state-to-state.) In researching the accuracy of this 1:5 ratio, statistics are either unavailable or obscure. There are so many varying points along an adoption timeline that it may, in fact, be just too difficult to accurately track a reversed decision. Regardless, I don't think you need to be embedded in the situation to acknowledge that a woman considering adoption would vacillate or even abandon her plan.

Another apprehension was related to the complications posed by the biological father who, sometimes, is unaware of the pregnancy and/or adoption plans. Even when cognizant, he could silently oppose and object at a later date. Or he may decide to author a different set of terms for the adoptive parents than what the biological mother had proposed.

Our impression was that too many stars had to properly align for a successful domestic adoption and felt it was too precarious a path to travel, especially with our track record.

And yes, I admit that I formed some misconceptions from watching too many made-for-television movies about adoptions gone awry with cinematic hyperbole.

We also did not want to compete with couples in dire straits, who lived a nightmare of struggles as they failed to grow their family. But when we took a breath and finally allowed objectivism to provide a crucial reality check, we realized that we too reside among these longing couples. So perhaps we shouldn't rule it out so quickly. And when facing the unobstructed truth, we had to accept the lack of dwindling options. During the past year alone, several previously prominent foreign adoption programs were either closing or significantly reducing their profiles. And after our experience in Morocco, did we even want to venture overseas again? Sadly, the answer is a firm "no."

Maybe it is time to take a second look at domestic adoption.

While vacillating with this reevaluation, we receive an email from Ben, the next door neighbor I briefly conversed with while being loaded onto a gurney in the middle of the night. Each sentence is written atop a bed of eggshells, careful not to tread too forcefully. Ben supplies us with the contact information for his friend, Jeff, who had two recent and successful domestic adoptions through a west coast adoption law center.

During this time, practically everyone we know is tripping over one another with contacts who've adopted children: relatives, friends, neighbors, coworkers, friends of friends, even relatives of friends. Although grateful for all of their kindness, we just aren't ready to reconsider domestic adoption. Maybe this alternative route of adopting through a law center instead of an agency is what piques my interest, but something inexplicable draws me to Jeff's story.

I begin composing an email to him, but with frustrated hand, delete the entire message. This happens three times. While it may sound ridiculous to ring my hands over a simple email seeking nothing beyond general information, there is such a profound chasm of danger lingering within these words. This email is representative of a hope so brittle—and especially now, it is such an explosive emotion to permit entry. But during a single moment of serenity I compose a message to Jeff that I don't want to delete. And when I feel not necessarily brave, but just brave enough, I press "send."

## SHEER WILLPOWER

Within this email, I introduce myself, mention our mutual friend, and vaguely detail our trials in Morocco and ventures with IVF. Then I offer a slew of apologies and disclaimers about the series of intrusive questions that follow. Below is a sample of what I bombard this total stranger with:

What compelled you to select a law center over a typical agency?
Were you paired with a representative? If so, did you feel supported by them?
How long was it before you were matched?
Were you interviewed by the birth mothers?
Did you have any referrals fall through?
Are your adoptions opened or closed?
What advice would you offer us in moving forward?

And the awkward question not found anywhere on the law center's website: cost. Intrusive and possibly offensive, but I ask if he is open to sharing a general price range.

That same evening, I receive a reply from Jeff. It begins, "Hi Lauri. Of course I don't mind... feel free to ask anything, anytime. I will try to answer any questions you have." He composed four pages worth of detail rich with helpful information, replete with answers to each of my questions. Jeff gives specifics on the process, the pros and cons, and valued advice. But the greatest gift Jeff imparts in this email wasn't written, but abstractly inferred through his words: *hope*. He even includes a photo of his two beautiful daughters.

A few days later, I walk down to Russ's office to ask if he's ready. Russ nods and rises, taping a pre-written note stating "On conference call" to his office door and closing it behind me. He pulls up a second chair for me and places the phone on speaker as he dials the number. We look at one another, take a deep breath, and clasp hands.

Her name is Eileen and we are preparing to initiate a phone consultation with her. She is an Adoption Consultant with the Law Center for Adoption (LCA). We have two oversized sticky notes loaded with questions for Eileen. This is just an information gathering session, I remind Russ. Experience has educated us. We are wiser and shrewder, and our BS radars are set to sensitive.

There are questions we could have posed in an email, but we wanted to detect the pauses, dissect the ambiguity, and sniff out the doubletalk. We had overlooked Murre's subtle red flags, and we refuse to be led astray again.

But Eileen is a consummate professional, devoid of seedy tactics. She answers our questions with a confident level of expertise and transparency.

Early that afternoon, Eileen emails us with a summarized outline of our call. Should we decide to move forward with LCA, she provides a contract and a financial breakdown of the cost. The price tag associated with marketing alone is a staggering $12,800. Digesting that five-digit figure is the moment it starts to feel real, and the decision is now upon us. Are we preparing to tighten the straps of our threadbare shoes once again and embark on another adventure? Will we finally reach the summit or does another avalanche lurk in the darkness ahead?

We realize our evening will involve a very engrossed and honest conversation, leading with one pivotal question: are we ready for this?

# SHEER WILLPOWER

## Crying in Public

*"There is a sacredness in tears. They are not the mark of weakness, but of power. They speak more eloquently than ten thousand tongues. They are the messengers of overwhelming grief, of deep contrition, and of unspeakable love."*
—*Washington Irving*

When it came to expressing vulnerabilities as an adolescent, I'm reminded of Superhero costumes from the 70s and 80s. They were essentially polyester onesies with cotton stuffing crammed into and sewn over biceps, triceps, and all muscular expanses of the human body, delivering the appearance of copious steroid use. I employed a similar disguise, padding my emotional muscles with rocks, an illusion that I was tough-shelled and vulnerably impervious. "Sticks and stones" was my mantra, but underneath that guise I was provoked by many words. And I distinctly recall the day when Macaulay Culkin blew my cover.

A blistering summer weekend left me stranded indoors. Seeking entertainment, I wandered into the family room where my parents were prying open the plastic casing of rented VHS movie. I sank into the empty loveseat, content to join them for this lighthearted flick. *My Girl* would sentimentally embark upon the reflection of lifelong friends, two kids growing up in the 70s. I had seen its trailer several times on

TV and there was not any indication of a sinister plot, no detectable undercurrent of looming, impending doom.* But how it misled! At just eleven years old, Macaulay Culkin's beloved character stumbles upon a hornet's nest and is stung—*to death*. Horrified by his passing, I averted my eyes from the television to peer out the window, a fruitless effort to pull myself from this fictional shock and back to reality. It failed and my emotions continued to ominously swell. I dug fingernails into fisted palms, but the physical pain was no barrier for the tears beginning to blur my vision. I silently recited the lyrics of my favorite Nirvana song ("Come as you are, as you were, as I want you to be..."), but I was reeling. I couldn't distract myself from the imminent devastation this death would have on his best friend, Vada. She already lost her mother and now she's about to learn that her best friend died (while out looking for her, no less)!

The dam burst and I erupted into a pool of teenage tears. I was wrecked. Superman met her kryptonite.

Whether suggested, implied, or simply imagined, I had equated emotional vulnerability with flaw. This caliber of flaw surpassed weakness and permanently docked itself at character-deficiency. Like a chipped teacup, I was damaged, unusable and pushed to the dark corner of a kitchen cupboard. Now that I was exposed, witnessed by the two people I continually strived to impress, I felt instantly shackled to my new persona. However, an unexpected reaction followed. My parents gently beckoned me to sit between them on the couch. There was no mocking, no disgust, no condescension. Instead, they threw their arms around me and we three shared our grief while cuddling under a blanket for the remainder of the film. An epiphany

---

\* See for yourself: https://www.youtube.com/watch?v=DqGv6qfHlmc

soon struck: emotions do not denote weakness; rather, they simply confirm a pulse. Lesson learned.

Fast-forward twenty years and life doles complexities beyond a fictional character's death. Although I still believe in the revelation I had at fifteen, it's difficult to fully embrace emotional vulnerability. And during my quest to motherhood, my challenge became the spectacle of crying in public. I may not have burst into tears over, say, a conversation about porcupine quill toxicity (which is, of course, a hot topic in most circles), but I would frequently lose composure in the waiting room of the IVF clinic. After the discovery of my ectopic pregnancy and the compilation of problems exposed during each appointment, I could no longer feign a stiff upper lip. Fear and anxiety were at the wheel, and each passing minute in the waiting room hammered any scrap of serenity that remained. I would draw my legs up onto the seat of the chair, shriveling into a tight fetal position. With a magazine shielding my face, I would quietly sob, decimating an entire packet of tissues.

As detailed throughout my journey, there were other instances of cracking: sitting before Rania at the Moroccan orphanage; splayed in radiology while a heavily pregnant sonographer analyzed my ectopic pregnancy; behind the closed door of Ziyan's office when he kindly suggested I go home. Despite my best efforts, I was merely armed with an umbrella during a monsoon.

When unable to pull the reins of emotional grief, a trifecta of cruel elements simultaneously competes for your attention: the source for the onslaught of tears, the embarrassment caused by this public display, and the wretched shame from an inability to steel oneself. I have often wondered if others are equipped with better functioning grief digestive systems. Perhaps it's akin to one person recovering from a concussion after several weeks while another with an identical injury requires numerous months for a full recuperation. Maybe it has everything to do with biological prewiring. Or emotional recovery may be based on upbringing and familial support. Perhaps it can be attributed to prayer or meditation. Maybe the answer lies in speaking freely about it or taking a vow of silence to never address it again. Regardless of technique and application, just as a physical injury necessitates attention and recovery, emotional trauma does too.

I've concluded that as we run at different speeds, our grief is uniquely processed. My personal antidote permits self-nurturing. I mourn as needed, unabatedly and unapologetically. I am the physician of my emotional health and if a purge is prescribed, it is fulfilled.

The grief specific to a miscarriage is a peculiar occurrence. When learning of a pregnancy, an instant and overwhelming joy is experienced from something intangible, both unseen and unfelt. But when unceremoniously stripped of it, when the being you sheltered and shared your body with suddenly vanishes, your new identity as an expectant mother is destroyed.

To some, it is logically and neatly explained away as the body ridding itself of a biological imperfection. But to those who've pained to reach the milestone of pregnancy, it is no less than absorbing the news of a death. It is the death of the future life you had imagined for yourself.

And it is grieved. Deeply.

But I discover that grief tenders a gift for its trouble, because the aftermath of each episode often presents a clarity, like an offering from the gods. It's as if I have been handed a pair of eyeglasses after years of viewing life with poor vision. I can see with crisp precision and revived color. These glimpses are individualistic and experienced at varying degrees, but one of my greatest personal revelations is an unanticipated degree of inner strength. I dusted myself off after falls from which I never would have envisioned rising. Renowned writer and professor, Joseph Campbell, stated, "The Universe always strikes you at your weakest point because that's what most needs strengthening." I believe that philosophy holds great merit.

If granted entrance, a powerful knowledge of self-discovery reveals itself through tragedy, and inexplicably, enlightenment is found in its lesson.

# Analysis Paralysis

The remainder of my workday is laced with introspective noise. We've been gradually warming to the idea of domestic adoption and position LCA as a top contender to facilitate it. But doubt creeps in, blanketing my budding confidence.

I have not yet come to terms with my failed instinct when selecting Murre. Lilith spoke with elegance and poise but it was right there, camouflaged within the margins. Her duplicitous nature delivered a sales pitch with saccharine and manipulation. How had I missed it? I'm plagued by a looming fear, forcing my hand in its examination: Did I really overlook it or glibly opt to look past? Or worse, was I actually aware but sought the outcome so desperately that I reasoned it away? These are such fundamentally imperative questions for me to address, yet I have no clear connection to their answers.

However, I accept that unveiling the truth holds no real value because each prospect inflicts suspicion on my ability to constructively assess and reach a decision.

*I* had selected Murre.
*I* suggested we chance this newly-minted Morocco program.
*I* agreed to travel to Morocco despite the internal warnings when no

information was provided about the children.
*I* chose IVF, the specific clinic, and the preference for natural cycle.

I had made countless decisions with zero victories. If these results were transferred to a professional environment, I'd be well-acquainted with my local unemployment office.

Russ advocates moving forward with LCA and is prepared to sign the contract. But I find myself gripped with uncertainty and stew inside my mind for days.

I'm not convinced that I can make this choice with unobstructed objectivism. I may have broken the internal meter operating my logic. I question my own intuition and grow suspect of my judgment. Somehow, I need to restore and rebuild from within.

It's quite easy to retreat after a series of failures. A shrug of the shoulders and defeated sigh accompanying the words spoken with dramatic finality, "Well, I tried." No one can argue that we didn't put forth the effort. Our numerous attempts were met with a multitude of dead-ends and crushing letdowns.

But failure continually offers the opportunity for resilience.

The Rubik's Cube presents multiple facets and innumerable configurations. Its user can be left frustrated with a jumbled mess of erroneous results posing a seemingly undefeatable challenge. But a solution surely exists, for the brightly colored cube *and* for me. Both require twists and turns paired with an acute level of focus and patience to its discovery. I thrive on analogies and this is just another to assist in propelling me forward.

So I break through the doubt, crack open my laptop, and settle in for a session of extensive research. My first objective is to investigate adopting through a law center. It wasn't until Ben's email that I even understood this to be a viable option. I had believed they were wholly devoted to legalizing adoptions after the selection of adoptive parents by biological parents. I didn't realize they could facilitate the marketing, vetting, matching, and post-placement visits (performed by a social worker following the baby's "placement" with his/her adoptive family) as well. Their operations closely parallel an adoption agency so I set off to examine the differences.

Unfortunately, this was not a straightforward task. When comparing the two, the majority of information my investigation uncovers is from either resource. That doesn't exactly yield an impartial viewpoint. Additionally, I struggle to separate fact from fiction. For instance, while LCA specifically outlines their post-placement arrangement, other sources distinctly state that law centers do not offer this service. However, Jeff confirms their involvement with post-placement plans for both of his adoptions. I also find law centers, law firms, and facilitators are often used interchangeably, blurring the lines of distinctively different operations.

I am not advocating one over another, as a simple internet search will result in a volatile display of opinions and personal experiences, supporting and opposing each. In fact, the volume of available information on agencies and law centers leads me plummeting down the rabbit hole's endless depths. A Google search returns more than 600,000 links for the word pairing "adoption agencies," while "adoption law center" generates over 46,000 links. And the lone "adoption" produces a dizzying 192,000,000 sources for both humans and animals alike.

The massive quantity of online data related to adopting a child, and the time invested in its research, should qualify hopeful parents for an advanced degree. I would spend an exhaustive six hours fixed to a computer screen researching option $Q$, gradually building and nearly

## SHEER WILLPOWER

solidifying confidence in its selection. And then one fateful last click results in a stunning and horrific account, essentially invalidating all prior work. It's like spending the entire day meticulously aligning dominos and with the placement of that last piece, a finger's accidental twitch sends them collapsing onto one another. It is easy to find yourself in a continual loop of disorienting analysis and a demoralizing state of limbo.

We really had performed ample due diligence with LCA, well-exceeding our research with Murre. We now held LCA to a higher standard, aware of the questions we naively neglected to ask, certain to address them this time. I grew more adept at reading within those margins.

I conclude that there are compelling advantages as well as concerns along both paths and no one course guarantees a successful adoption. In the end, we have to trust not only our research, but most importantly, ourselves—a concept that has reintroduced itself repeatedly. And I think I'm ready to do that once again.

Taking another monumental step forward, we sign the contract with LCA.

That evening, Russ and I celebrate our decision over hot plates of chicken teriyaki and lo mein at our favorite Asian-fusion restaurant. When we crack open our fortune cookies, mine prophetically reads, "Don't be afraid to take that big step." Before vacating our table, I tuck it inside my wallet.

LAURI M. VELOTTA-RANKIN

## Another Year Passes

*"Real happiness is not the result of making dreams come true. It is the result of sorrow, sadness and loss. Yes, you read that right. The happiest people I have met are people who have experienced sorrow and climbed their way out of it. Happiness of this kind is hard to mimic any other way. When you feel this type of happiness, trees can make you happy. The wind can make you smile. The flowers can bring tears."* —Christina Rasmussen

That December, I turn thirty-four years old. When I inspect myself in the mirror, I see how the last year has taken a considerable toll on my fleeting youth. It is reflected in the deepened horizontal lines on my forehead and a healthy sprouting of pepper along my hairline. The stress has thinned me, with the hollowing of cheeks that adds years to my face. Despite this recent physical wear, one positive sign of aging is present, found within those fine lines around the corners of my eyes. They have been fashioned by a lifetime devoted to relentless smiles.

Growing our family has been the greatest battle either of us has ever confronted. An unexpected, multi-layered fight has been unleashed, striking us physically, emotionally, and financially. That being said, life's innumerable wonders unveil themselves daily and I'd be a wretched fool to overlook the marvels of this bounty. I am in good physical health, as are my loved ones. Russ and I maintain a happy marriage, brought even closer through the hardships we've faced. We're surrounded by an army of friends and family consistently restoring our morale. We are both well-employed with a comfortable level of fiscal security. We readily supply our table with food of our own selection. We can indulge in superfluous purchases from time to time. We do not live in fear of personal safety or persecution. And when I pause and peek outside the confines of my life, I am witness to expressions of human decency, compassionate acts, and remarkable benevolences.

The holidays and impending New Year carries a steadfast recognition of these fortunes, along with a revitalization of hope and reconstructed perseverance. I'm fully cognizant of the fact that failure is inevitable, as I've had the misfortune of colliding with it several times along this journey. But I won't fixate on what lies behind me or drown in its despair because this song has yet another verse.

LAURI M. VELOTTA-RANKIN

# Caffeinated Splendor

Russ and I enter our favorite coffee shop (the one where I found the "Act of Kindness" earrings) and locate a table for two. While Russ places our order, I proceed to spread out, sort through, and prioritize the paperwork that will expedite our adoption. The sooner we complete all requirements, the quicker our profile is placed online for birth mothers to view. We've now entered a mental marathon and begin chipping away form after lengthy form. Some of them are familiar from our foreign adoption and pinprick my heart, but I refocus, identifying this new venture as a fresh start.

One of the principal differences between domestic and foreign adoption is that while the latter is restricted to placement and availability, the former is largely dependent upon marketing efforts. We're provided sample photos of adoptive parents and I'm transported back to the mall's Glamour Shots photography studio of the early 90s. Smoky photos of women covered the store windows: a fisted hand placed beneath her chin, head tilted to the right, and a distanced, contemplative expression. Many of these adoption photos look uncomfortably posed while some appear blatantly staged: hopeful-dad on bended knee tying a child's shoelace as a bystander just happens to snap a photo with him smiling warmly into the lens, mid-action. It resembles a magazine ad for toothpaste or men's khakis.

## SHEER WILLPOWER

Michelle, a media specialist contacted us yesterday, requesting that we "schedule a 15-20 minute phone consultation." There are strict guidelines we must follow regarding our submitted photos. As a precursor to this call, we receive an email with an attached file entitled "Media Requirements." It includes the necessity of over sixty photos, detailing the exact number to be taken as a couple and individually. "Action shots" are necessary as well, depicting engagement in enjoyed activities. Professional photography is permitted, but if not utilized, tips have been included for the amateur, like the advantages of shooting on a cloudy day and when best to use a flash. Directions include removing sunglasses and limiting photos where baseball hats adorn heads. (This makes me chuckle, as I imagine every balding man releasing an audible groan at that restriction.) The packet concludes with a statement reminding of their expertise and familiarity with birth mother preferences, the emphasis clearly denoting an adherence to these rules. In other words, do not bother to scoff, question, or critique their well-established instructions because they know what they're doing. We get it and will gladly abide.

We also receive sample letters to birth mothers where prospective adoptive parents begin with sentiments like "We are honored by your consideration," "Thank you for your bravery," and "Words cannot express." When viewing the many online profiles of these adoptive couples, their particular selection of words may vary, but they all possess identical frameworks. And how could they not? Being considered to raise someone's child is an extraordinarily humbling honor. To choose adoption exemplifies fierce courage and the gravity of a biological mother's decision exceeds all words.

Selecting the right language for this letter to our future child's biological mother is intense and massively challenging. What can express an accurate level of appreciation while attempting to understand the difficulty that must be involved in that deliberation? (I even cringe at my use of the words "appreciation" and "difficulty," as neither seems to give adequate justice.) How does one begin to compose such a letter? Although it's crucial in our paperwork submission, we agree to reflect on it separately and table it for the time being.

Instead, we tackle the questionnaire and its intricate dissection of our lives. As directed, we describe our home, pets, and neighborhood. We detail the specifics of a three day weekend. What do we hope to teach our child? We're instructed to outline what we plan to divulge about his or her birth parents as well as explain the relationship we want with them. We state why we have chosen adoption, how we met, why we were attracted to one another, the make-up of our personalities, the hobbies that capture our attention, and so on. Some answers easily flow from fingers to keyboard while others require significant thought.

We account for our love of kayaking in the summer, skiing during the winter, and a shared pleasure found in simple things, like taking our dog on a walk. We explain how we hope to teach our child to demonstrate kindness towards all, foster his or her intellectual exploration, remain positive and tenacious through trials, and discover the impact of volunteerism. Utilizing words like happy, safe, and sheltered, we communicate the celebration of family and how we have always felt loved.

We essentially share our most personal thoughts, delicate hopes, and precious memories that strangers will comb through, all of them passing by with one exception, one woman lingering longer in consideration.

After an extensive morning of work, my mind wanders as I notice a mother and her two young daughters occupy the table besides us. The girls appear to be around four and six years old and excitedly communicate in Spanish. After a few moments of conversation between the three, the younger child turns to face the window behind her chair.

## SHEER WILLPOWER

"Papi!" she exclaims as she catches sight of a man approaching from the parking lot. Sheer delight erupts and the girls furiously knock on the glass to attract his attention. When he takes notice, a wide smile spreads across his face and he waves a gloved hand back at them. His reaction sends them into a frenzy of giggles. Before he can even place both feet inside the establishment, he's greeted at the door with tight hugs from these two, doting little humans.

The movie *Love Actually* is bookended with actual video footage of loved ones reuniting at Heathrow Airport.[*] We witness repeated instances of warm embraces laced with elation. There are kisses, laughter, tears, and closed eyes directed skyward, as if blissfully thanking the fates that brought them together. Despite the mere split seconds spent observing people I've never met hug one another, I have never made it through either end of the movie without dabbing at tears. And while this coffee shop scene unfolds before me, I recognize the brilliance behind the decision not to employ actors for these reunions. The authenticity simply can't be manufactured, no matter how Oscar-worthy the performance.

As I watch this coffee shop reunion, goosebumps cover my arms and I try to yawn away the tears. Several people weave around this father with his two daughters, hot coffees in hand, some carrying laptop bags or newspapers, or busy in conversation with a device firmly pressed against an ear. They've likely missed the unfolding of this tender moment. But I see this father's eyes sparkle, the love in his touch, and the distinctive joy his presence has brought his daughters. I wonder if it's been awhile since they've seen one another or if they parted several hours earlier. Whatever their story, this display of familial love moves me, and I feel the imperativeness of our quest.

---

[*] https://www.youtube.com/watch?v=cUoxXpqof8A

After working for almost three hours, Russ suggests a break. With forks in hand, we pluck at an oversized blueberry muffin and sip fresh coffees. He teases me about my jitters the night prior. When writing our first check to LCA, I made an error and immediately delivered it to the shredder. So I carefully tore a second blank check at the perforated line and put pen to paper. But in misspelling a word, it too became paper clippings. It was mastered by the third try, secured inside an envelope, and with a trembling hand, placed in the mailbox.

# A Turbulent Take-Off

The relationship with "Aunt" Catherine, our local social worker during the Moroccan adoption, continues as we reach out to her seeking a modification to our home study. At the fee of one hundred dollars, she revises it to reflect the change in venue from foreign to domestic. Before sending a notarized copy to LCA, we catch a typo on page four in a section entitled "Financial Resource" asserting that our monthly expenses near a staggering $50,000! We notify Catherine and she's quick to correct the error. But it's an uncomfortable reminder of her lack of attention to critical detail.

Catherine explains that she'll play a more active role in our domestic adoption than she did when directed overseas, reemerging once the baby's birth mother legally consents to the adoption post-birth. Additionally, she will coordinate with the hospital's social worker to ensure the baby is discharged into our care. Catherine will also administer one final assessment, the post-placement visit. It will occur in our home several weeks after we return with the baby—rather, "your baby," as she repeatedly states during our in-person meeting.

When this language was used the first time we sought adoption, I'd break out into a goofy smile. But now, as I listen to Catherine rattle off this list, mapping out these future requirements while referring to this child as ours, I can't help but feel an edge of discomfort. While it's customary to maintain sealed lips when trying to conceive, occasionally followed by quiet whispers revealing early signs of pregnancy to a select few, we exemplify the antithesis of these societal norms. We instead march forward with heavy foot, smashing together cymbals and speaking in boisterous voices while planning something nonexistent, an idea no greater than a hope. So I travel this curious world of adoption with numbed, artificial excitement because I'm really too damn scared to acknowledge its full presence in my life.

Catherine wishes us better luck this time, and with that, we provide LCA our new home study. Like expectant parents, we too amass items marked with ABC's and 1, 2, 3's. But ours relate to the plethora of alphanumeric documents necessitated for adoption. The I-600A is a United States Citizenship and Immigration Services (USCIS) form that grants clearance when run against the FBI's various databases. A requirement for both foreign and domestic adoption, we find it among the old Moroccan paperwork and are relieved to see that ours are still valid. But our bubble bursts when LCA informs us that we'll have to reapply with USCIS because our clearances expire in a little over one month. It had taken more than six weeks to receive feedback the year prior, so the setback is disappointing. Assuming the processing time hasn't miraculously accelerated, we're now left wondering if this will delay the execution of our online profile. But Michelle reassures us, stating that if this form is the only missing document, our profile will be live with a theoretical asterisk indicating that our full approval is pending.

We've willingly engaged ourselves in a sprint, determined to rapidly complete all tasks related to this adoption. Deep consideration and a meticulous review of every written word assure no haphazard decisions. We are so securely cemented in this commitment that we're practically rendered immobile. Is less introspection needed when the past several years have been spent enduring a battle to become parents? I waver on this assessment because at times, it feels like we've purposely fastened ourselves to the two rails of steel train tracks. With the awareness of imminent, oncoming trains, each item crossed off out list loosens the knotted rope that binds us. Maybe expediting the paperwork has nothing to do with the certainty of adoption, but rather, its representation. The preparation manifests the haunts of a ghost, an unrelenting wound of our history. Perhaps we perceive our online profile as a tangible measurement and final deliverance from these tracks.

The weekend arrives and Russ and I seat ourselves at the computer to begin sorting through all the photos we've taken over the past year. We pull several into a new folder labeled "Adoption Profile Photos," but too few seem suitable for inclusion and we definitely lack the volume LCA demands. We decide to visit our favorite local park with a camera and tripod, bringing along several changes of clothes (as specified in the Media Requirements document details).

We look like a pair of indecisive teenagers picking the appropriate outfit for a first date—except we must select numerous items. We model and toss clothes around our bedroom, deeming few good enough for these all-important profile photos. We try to psychoanalyze a birth mother's preference: not too dull, but not too trendy. Holding a dress up to my chest, I half-tease, "Does this portray me as fun, yet responsible?" Russ reassures that it does, but I know he doesn't have any more of a clue than me. He wonders if a plaid button-down is suitable. Although honesty warrants a shrug, I tell him it's perfect. I debate wrapping one of my handmade scarves around my neck since I listed knitting as a hobby. Or do I opt for more rugged wear, as indicated in our love for the outdoors? How do we give the appearance that we didn't try so hard while being fully aware of the fact that these are the most important photos of our lives? I have never put more thought into clothing as I am now, and I regret judging the posed photos of other couples. If there were less on the line, this would surely register as comical.

We finally settle on a few outfits. I drop a handful of earrings and necklaces into a small pocket of my bag and sling it over my shoulder. As we open the door to leave, Chase bounds towards us and we plead with him to *stay* in an effort to keep drool stains and white hair off our pants. His whines in protest, but obeys. Russ loads the car with our kayaks, his bike, and my roller blades, and we set off to smile, dance, and pose for the camera.

And yes, I wear the knitted scarf while Russ dons the plaid shirt. My hair and make-up are presented no differently than usual. We really strive to project authenticity despite the unnatural circumstance of taking sixty photos in a single day. We begin with the couples shots, seated together on a boulder overlooking a pond. We fumble with the camera's timer and multiple-shots feature, and before long, we're in hysterics over our blunders. Ironically, these produce some of the best photos of the day.

After four wardrobe changes and driving all over town to photograph ourselves against scenic backdrops, our camera's SD card is loaded with over one hundred photos. And we are exhausted. My mouth aches from the repetition of compulsory smiles.

We head home and begin the process of weeding through each image. I'm reminded of an episode of *Friends* when Chandler's smile morphs into an exaggerated grimace as he labors to manifest a natural expression during an engagement photo shoot. I feel his struggle now as I can easily identify the photos with my forced smiles.

## SHEER WILLPOWER

Regardless, it was a successful day and we proudly supply LCA with all sixty of our pictures, neatly organized into categories and subcategories. We even add a folder containing several extra photos if needed. With chests puffed at the completed task, we place our sealed CD inside the mailbox, ready for delivery to LCA.

Later that week, Michelle emails us with the following news: "While we have some really great photos we can use on your web profiles, we are going to need a few more..." Our gaffes include wearing the same outfit in all the close-ups and having my sunglasses propped atop my head in one set of photos, which is prohibited. Admittedly, this seems a little nitpicky. We knew we couldn't cover our eyes with sunglasses, but I never realized having them perched atop my head would fall under that same umbrella. Michelle also references the photos "with your daughter" and seeks more to represent our "family dynamic." We immediately let her know that we included a few photos with our niece, not our child, and express concern that this could be a birth mother's assumption as well. Asking if she can eliminate those photos from consideration, she agrees that would be a good idea. Lastly, Michelle references the photos of Russ riding his bike, supplied as his action shots. She doesn't like that his head is covered... by a bicycle helmet. The action shots are meant to depict our interests and one of his is cycling. This restriction abrades a bit more. Aren't we shirking personal responsibility by taking new photos of him riding without the helmet he always wears? And putting this in perspective, they will likely select one or two of these action shots to reside among countless hair-baring photos. Do we really need to orchestrate another simulated bike-riding venture? But I'm reminded of their statements about expertise and knowing what birth mothers want to see in regards to photos. Taking several deep breaths on this critique, we let her know that we'll supply photos of Russ standing beside his bike with helmet in hand, not on his head.

We quickly agree to reshoot and supply them with another CD. Russ will be traveling overseas for a business trip in two days so we head outside with the camera that afternoon. By evening, we're standing at the counter of our neighborhood UPS store mailing the new images.

Our online profile is launched on three different websites. Pregnant women considering (or having already decided upon) adoption can now view our photos, read our birth mother letter and learn about our lives. It's wonderful and daunting and exciting and scary, because now, we simply wait.

I remember the feeling of victory when we completed months of hard work required for our Moroccan adoption and swallow my fear. This time will be different. I have no sane choice but to believe that.

One of the websites includes a private visitor counter, enabling us to see the number of times our profile has been viewed. Access to this feature is fantastic and we gleefully watch as our hits climb. However, it doesn't take long for us to recognize the adverse effect of this gift. Enthusiasm transforms into discomfort because although these numbers grow, our phone fails to ring. Each day becomes a battle of wills, as I sit at my desk in the morning, silently promising a boycott of that counter. But as the hours creep, my focus wanes—and with it, my determination. As much as I want to ignore its existence, I succumb to curiosity and check often.

# With Tempered Emotions

*"I dwell in possibility." –Emily Dickinson*

In an effort to retain sanity, I've drastically modified my expectations. With the Moroccan adoption and pregnancies, I felt invigorated, like a child dancing away the countdown to Christmas. I observed progress with cheery enthusiasm, sitting atop a stack of pins and needles awaiting good news. But now all I feel are the pricks from those pointy ends. I equate it to the beloved but thickheaded Charlie Brown always trusting Lucy's guarantee of a firmly grasped football. He and I both, repeatedly, find ourselves laid-out on our backsides seeing stars. This time I vow to alter my game plan. I'm still in the game, but I've plotted my defense and refuse to invest energy in Lucy's empty promises. I no longer readily share our adoption plans. I don't read adoption blogs or browse websites with baby-related merchandise. I definitely will not purchase anything that signifies impending parenthood. I hold my future as a parent at arms-length. Of course that is where I long to exist and we're making every effort to reach it. But at this precise moment, I opt to shelter myself from potential catastrophe. Perhaps I'll be confident enough to free these emotions when we're matched, when we hear the birth mother's voice, when she declares this child to be ours. But for now, I'm committing to sentiments of neutrality. This is my freshly scripted self-preservation strategy.

Eileen sends us an email commending our successful completion of LCA's paperwork. She mentions that this abrupt halt likely feels strange, and while reading her words, I find myself smiling and nodding in agreement. When you've spent months pedaling hard and finally breach that finish line, you're left idling for an indefinite period. It's an odd transition because you feel like you need to keep moving forward but you can't. We went from being completely responsible for everything in this process to having no control whatsoever. It's invigorating and nerve-wracking at the same time.

Eileen states that once a birth mother expresses interest in our profile and completes their requirements, LCA will notify us. She details the extensive documentation for birth mothers, including medical forms to authenticate pregnancy and prenatal records. LCA will not enter into a contract without it. Sadly, there are people who prey on the vulnerability of hopeful parents and working with an agency or law center often weeds these out because of their rigid verification practices.

Now that our media profile is complete, the baton is handed to Lorayne, an Adoption Advisor. Our communications are entirely limited to email, but she's been extremely informative and responsive to our inquiries.

Our adoption profile has been online for two weeks when Russ is summoned to Kuwait on another work-related venture. He leaves on a Sunday morning and will be back in ten days. The following Tuesday, I'm returning home after work when I notice my cell phone blinking with a voice mail. I ascend my driveway, shift the gear to park, unclip my seatbelt, and take a closer look. No more than four seconds pass from the moment I noticed the indicator light to the time I viewed the phone's screen. But that minuscule expanse of time permits a typhoon of thoughts to cross my mind: How did I miss this call? Was it set to vibrate? Maybe it went directly to voice mail. Was my music too loud? Did Russ need to reach me? And the foremost question that causes my heart to skip a beat every time my phone rings: *What if LCA is calling?* I admonish myself for the instant catapult to this prospect, but sooner or later, I hope to be right.

The missed call is from an unprogrammed number, but I do recognize the area code and know that our only contact in that state is indeed LCA. My heart races as I key my voice mail code. I hear Lorayne's voice for the first time. She wants us to know that there is a possible match for us, but warns that it's not in complete alignment with our parameters. She asks that I give her a call back to discuss the details. Still seated in the driver's seat of my car, I immediately return her call. But after several unanswered rings, her voice mail launches and I leave an anxious message.

I'm now pacing inside my home, unable to still my body and mind. Chase prances around me, perceptive of my quiet and nervous excitement. Promising him a long walk later that afternoon, I take him to the backyard to relieve himself. I spend the next hour scaling the walls of speculation, wondering the cause of this potential misalignment. There are not only a host of reasons but a scale within each, ranging from benign to dire. There's no diverting my mind from this matter, I just think about how my entire life could change with this one call. But then again, I've said that many times before.

It's just after two in the morning in Kuwait and I debate phoning Russ. I laugh aloud at the coincidence of these the middle of the night calls when Russ travels to this particular country. While my last call resulted in an immediate return home due to my ectopic pregnancy, this one could possibly be the greatest of his life. Our life-altering moments now center around his visits to the Middle East. Should I wait to contact him until I learn more from Lorayne? I waver, and opt against waking him until I know the facts.

Ensuring the ringer is set at its highest volume, my cell is never further than two feet from me. Within the hour, my phone trills. It's Lorayne and after a quick exchange of greetings, I ask her if she can please just tell me what places this match on shaky ground before conversing about anything else. If this is a deal-breaker, I'd like to know upfront. With a leveled voice, she explains that we were selected by one of their birth mothers, but the discrepancy is due to the baby being…

Hispanic.

I pause to absorb her words, then ask if she can please repeat herself because I don't connect the discrepancy's association with ethnicity. Lorayne references LCA's document related to racial identification and states that we hadn't selected Hispanic.

I think back to the day Russ and I sat at the kitchen table to address this form, and how bizarre it felt to have an opinion, or even a preference, in regards to the child's ethnicity. We felt this was something that should happen organically. If a woman, pregnant with a half Thai and Dominican baby, chooses us, then *yes*. If the baby were half Dutch and Malaysian, *yes*. Equal fifths Irish, Portuguese, Angolan, Native American, and Filipino, *yes*. The exact racial make-up wasn't for us to decide. We would be honored to parent, period. So placing check marks beside the numerous conglomerations of options was an uneasy task. And the volume of racial variations was extensive. Lorayne said that while we had selected many races mixed with Hispanic, we had not checked the box for an exclusively Hispanic baby.

## SHEER WILLPOWER

My heart SOARS with elation! This was the sole reason for Lorayne's tentative message. There were no problems with the baby's health or apprehensions about the birth mother. This issue is a non-issue.

Now it's time to wake Russ. After gathering some more information, I ask Lorayne if I can call her back in a few minutes because I want to reach Russ and share this unbelievable news. It is nearing 3AM in Kuwait. His phone connects with the sound of an international ring, and when he answers, my first words are, "Everything is okay. Actually, I have great news. Honey, *we've been matched!*" I proceed to tell him about Lorayne's hesitance and Russ reacts with the same confusion about the baby's ethnicity. We laugh together, relieved by the unveiling. The birth mother is due in three short months. And I then divulge that the baby is a girl.

It's nearly impossible to find the words to accurately describe this moment, but it's a muddled concoction of excitement, relief, and fear. The last noun casts a shadow over the others, yet it's the reality of adoption. Although this birth mother has selected us, she is at liberty to change her mind and parent her baby. We soon learn that she will have ten days after the baby is born to take her child back. And for most, if not all, of that time, the baby would be in our care. Regardless, we allow ourselves to privately celebrate. We proceed with a new mantra: cautious optimism.

Lorayne emails us photos of a beautiful, vibrant, pregnant teenager named Leah. While Leah looks thoughtful in some images, most are selfies, playfully sticking out her tongue or posing sweetly with her boyfriend, Thomas, the baby's biological father. He is as handsome as Leah is pretty. But it is the third series of photos that really takes our breath away. Those images show a newly-toothed toddler gleefully smiling for the camera. She is Leah and Thomas's sixteen month old daughter, Angelique. What little hair she's grown is gathered at the top of her head, secured by a blue tie, while the remainder falls in dark ringlets behind her ears. She is simply precious. Angelique and Leah's unborn child will be full, biological siblings, and we feel that we've just been given a sneak peek into the baby's possible appearance. Will a similar face have cheeks squeezed between Russ and mine in family photos? I still fear to let myself wade too deeply in these waters, but I do allow the thought to linger, just for a moment.

Some birth parents select the adoptive parents and then proceed to take a giant step back, while others request in-person visits. Leah and Thomas find comfortable grounds somewhere in middle and elect to speak with us over the phone. And Lorayne has scheduled this for tomorrow. She will facilitate a four-way phone call, slightly complicated since Russ is still working in Kuwait. Lorayne tells us she will remain present for the call's duration, asking questions of both parties, helping to move the conversation along. She wants us to know that she will inquire about our relationship, how we plan to balance work and home life, and what will constitute as quality time with this child. She suggests that we ask Leah how she's been feeling and express our gratitude for her selection.

Lorayne then gently advises us that some couples who have parented a child together, like Leah and Thomas, have changed their minds in the end, opting against adoption. We learn that Leah is hiding her pregnancy from family which Lorayne says increases the risk of the adoption falling through. She says that we "are the ones taking the leap of faith," and if uncomfortable with Leah's level of commitment after the call, to just let her know.

There is no guideline, research, or studying to adequately equip someone preparing for this kind of introduction. I actually feel physically weak in the knees. This is the first time I've ever had the sensation, as

## SHEER WILLPOWER

I thought it was merely an expression. I'm even struggling to type these exact words, as a distracted mind and trembling hands produce a multitude of careless errors.

Upon arriving home from work, I changed clothes. But I just found myself examining the shirt I'm wearing with no recollection of pulling it from a shelf and placing it on my body. I likely could not (and should not) safely operate a vehicle at this moment in time. I can barely withstand this fevered anticipation. My stomach is grumbling with hunger but I refrain from eating, convinced I'll vomit.

Now five minutes until the call and I'm pacing the kitchen, my shirt already saturated with sweat. I'm desperately seeking my inner calm, maniacally planning to hold it captive for at least the next fifteen minutes. "Ask Leah how she's feeling," and "express tremendous gratitude," I whisper aloud as reminders to myself. I can hardly believe what is set to transpire in three minutes. Is there any interview more intense than this? I think about our advocate, Lorayne, and how she will help guide us through this conversation. It's pretty incredible to be living such an emotionally-charged experience that will forever be ingrained in memory.

It is one minute until Lorayne calls and my heart is pounding. I turn my attention to my breath, slowly inhaling and exhaling.

The phone rings!

Lorayne connects our four phone lines spanning three states and two countries. Thomas was caught in evening traffic, so we speak exclusively with Leah. She presents a calm and upbeat manner, occasionally injecting laughter into the conversation. Flowing without bouts of awkward silence or tension, our chat is smoothly ushered along with Lorayne's assistance. As Leah discusses her pregnancy, the delighted squeal and chatter of Angelique is heard in the background. I wish

Russ were at my side so I could squeeze his hand in excitement. Thomas arrives before the call concludes and he asks if we can teach the baby how to play basketball, his favorite sport. It's a promise we easily agree to keep.

A few minutes after we end the call, Lorayne reaches me privately on my cell phone. She asks how we're feeling and conveys, "They loved you." She passes along their email addresses and phone numbers. Leah would like to keep in touch via email while Thomas prefers the occasional call. Lorayne then asks if she can share details with Leah and Thomas about our failure in Morocco and IVF-related complications. She wants them to know the extent of our difficulties and empower them with the knowledge they're personally responsible for our deliverance from it.

Lorayne suggests I reach out to Leah first, and I'm grateful for this opportunity to convey my thoughts, with less elevated nerves, through email. I really want nothing more than to connect with her! We are so fortunate for these open lines of communication, but they also require navigation through a possible minefield. I agonize over how to begin this message. I'm unsure of the proper tone and the words to accurately express an emphatic thank you. I'm also concerned about inadvertently misstating something or having my words taken out of context. And most gravely, I fear that getting this wrong could lead them to renounce us.

The more I stare at this blank email, motionless fingers hovering above the letters of my keyboard, the more I realize that Leah's feelings probably mirror mine. So I take a deep breath and release anxiety with its exhalation. I begin to type. I let her know how wonderful it was to speak with them and that we are so honored they selected us. I briefly outline our rocky, unsuccessful past to have a family and how we're overjoyed to welcome this child into our family. I end the mes-

## SHEER WILLPOWER

sage wishing her an early happy birthday, as I noticed from her paperwork, that it is less than two weeks away. Then I send it—to Russ in Kuwait. I want his discerning eye to analyze it from every angle before Leah reads it. He gives a thumbs up, soothing my nerves. And with a shaky finger, I press "Send."

An hour later, Leah replies. She states "...you are very welcome for the bundle of joy that is soon to come into your lives. I'm sure she'll take away all the pain that you guys have been through." She tells me that her obstetrician appointments are now scheduled every two weeks and she generously offers to provide updates following each one. She doesn't have to do this—she *wants* to.

She ends the message with a comment about the unseasonably warm winter weather they're having in her home state of New York. She playfully thanks global warming. Leah then provides cell phone numbers for both her and Thomas. I want to reach through the screen and embrace this young woman.

When learning that we'd been matched, I didn't cry. And I didn't cry after the phone call with Leah and Thomas. It is her email that allows me to release the stress, pain, frustration, and even fear. I cry, but these tears are new to me, as they're fat with untainted joy.

The following day, Lorayne sends an email reminding us that Leah has the right to request financial support. There are legal restrictions, but these can be related to assistance with rent and food, and these costs have been known to climb high. But Leah only asks for help with cab fare to and from her medical appointments. I'm touched by her very humble request and we immediately consent.

LAURI M. VELOTTA-RANKIN

# Haja Visits

*"We loved with a love that was more than love." —Edgar Allan Poe*

I think about the day ahead with genuine delight. My friend Kirsten, Haja's daughter-in-law, had sent me an email last week. She said Haja would be visiting from Morocco, and they've invited us over today. We're excited to not only see her again, but under a much-improved, less stressful set of circumstances.

I call downstairs to Russ asking if our camera's battery has a fresh charge, but he doesn't answer. I then hear the familiar complaint of the squeaky garden hose being unraveled a story below my bedroom window. I part the blinds and see Russ stretching it across the grass. Once he reaches the tree in the far corner of our yard, he saturates the earth beneath it. Russ has consistently tended to this lone maple tree. He mulched a dirt ring around its base for better water absorption and regularly sprays it with natural concoctions to protect against insects and disease. His care and attention are evident. Our tree now stands tall and strong. Its trunk has expanded in diameter and its branches are dotted with red buds, an early indication of Spring's impending arrival. Although still requiring basic care, this tree is not only healthy but thriving.

When Russ returns inside, I ask about the camera, and learn it's already charged and placed by the front door. We want to ensure we take a high-quality photo with Haja, as we plan to enlarge and frame it. A recent purchase of a collage photo frame was placed over our family room couch months ago and it's still populated with a series of attractive strangers. We intend to fill it with photos of our family, including images from our wedding and special documented events. When I had suggested including one with Haja, Russ enthusiastically replied, "Yes, she's part of our family!"

Kirsten answers the door and welcomes us into her home. As soon as I lay eyes on Haja, her warm smile floods my system with happiness. She rises from the couch and individually hugs us, planting kisses on our cheeks. Russ and I flank Haja, the three of us seated closely together. She had grabbed my hand when we first embraced and has yet to let go.

Although I am certainly old enough to be Haja's daughter, my love for her is reminiscent of my grandmother. The specifics of my childhood memories with her have generally faded but the residual feelings will never lose their luster. They are laced with merriment, protection, contentedness, and love. And there is something in Haja's spirit which closely parallels my grandmother. So sitting beside her, holding hands for an extended period of time doesn't feel awkward. Instead, it brings me immense comfort.

Haja's son, Adam, interprets for us when we inquire about the well-being of her family. We ask how Nabil is faring in school, commending his intelligence, maturity, and kindness. We mention exchanging emails with Yasmine and discuss her busy schedule as a doctor. We verbally dote on sweet baby Heba, learning about her most recent milestones.

Haja then opens our gift bag. Though certain we wanted to bring her a gift, we had no idea what it should be. But while in Morocco, she proudly showed me her embroidered work, so I thought she may enjoy the workings of a knitting loom. I include two balls of yarn, one newly purchased while the other belonged to my late grandmother. Kirsten asks which of the two it was, and I point to the fuzzy gray wool, speckled with hints of purple and gold. I explain that my grandmother was working on a knitting project when she passed away, and I've had the three precious remaining skeins. I felt it very fitting to give one to Haja. It was a kind of tribute to them both.

Adam toys with the camera settings while Kirsten closes the window's blinds behind us to avoid being backlit. Preparing for a photo, the three of us snuggle close together as a succession of flashes capture the moment. When it's time for us to leave, Haja holds our hands once again and blesses us with an Islamic prayer. Spending time with her again felt blissfully medicinal.

Several days later, Kirsten calls to ask if I can stop by and show Haja how to make a pom-pom for the hat she knitted on the loom. Kirsten tells me that Haja's been talking about additional knitting project she's planning once home, and I'm thrilled to hear she's found a hobby in our gift. After work that evening, I'm again seated next to Haja on the couch with hands busy in a task requiring no translation.

Haja visits with her son and his family annually so I'm comforted knowing we'll have the opportunity to see her again. And I think forward to the next year, wondering if we'll have this child for her to hold.

In the words of Haja's native tongue, "en shallah."

## A Delicate Balance

Perhaps it's one of the many stages in the adoptive parent's processing cycle, but I begin to deeply reflect upon my future child's biological mother. LCA has provided access to a scattered array of facts about her background, health, and current lifestyle, largely in the form of checkmarks she placed within boxes of their questionnaire. And though it merely offers the rough sketch to a vivid and elaborate painting, I peer through the keyhole of Leah's life.

Born to a seventeen year old, Leah is the oldest of seven children. Her mother is currently just one year older than me. Several of Leah's selections indicate her mother's struggle with both emotional and physical health. With six siblings following Leah's birth, and a father listed as unknown, I can only imagine that she bore a significant weight of responsibility for their care. A handwritten note besides one checked box discloses that one of her brother's had suffered with an unspecified mental illness. My eyes follow the column to the right and more of Leah's writing details his recent passing after a series of complications from pneumonia. She also reveals that a mass was removed from her right breast earlier this year. I already understand her young life to be unjustly and heartbreakingly rife with difficulties and my skin pricks with goosebumps. I feel an imaginary finger sternly tapping my shoulder, holding me accountable for my adolescent gripe of a life deemed too mundane. My ignorance yearned for severity in personal challenge and strife, shamefully unappreciative of my birth lottery's fortune. Conversely, in the midst of her youth, Leah endured a barrage of complexities too mature for any child's comprehension. Has she dreamed of the security and simplicity found within each page of my childhood's story, with a plot I habitually and thoughtlessly took for granted?

Leah now lives in a relative's home with her boyfriend and daughter. Although currently unemployed, she cites her "usual occupation" as a cashier and adds that Thomas is seeking a second job "to make ends meet." I wonder if she would still choose adoption if she had a cushy, middle-class lifestyle where purchasing a winter coat for her daughter didn't necessitate an assessment of funds. I also wonder if this decision is laced with the weight of heartache or centered within the pragmatism of relief. Perhaps it's as intertwined as drops of red food coloring released into a cup of water.

An unsettling thought stains my mind and it's impenetrable. Am I simply the beneficiary of her struggles?

Leah has recently graduated high school and early in our email correspondence, she expresses her hope to attend college someday. Ideally, she would like to study journalism. I reply with excitement, commending her writing skills and enthusiastically encouraging this goal's pursuit. As the hours pass, I think more about my reply and am riddled with guilt. My college fees were entirely and graciously funded by two parents who lovingly insisted on advancement channeled through a higher education. From my foolishly limited scope, I immediately assumed Leah's hesitancy was related to the self-discipline required for classes. I was advocating the achievement of her dream, utterly failing to recognize the huge financial burden attached to a degree, especially

## SHEER WILLPOWER

for a young family straining—as Leah's own words specified—"to make ends meet."

Before their delivery, I start intensive dissections of my emails, searching for commentary that could be misconstrued, comprise double-meanings, or expose some unintentional insensitivity. Spun into a state of written-paralysis, I'm left mentally exhausted when I finally do allow these messages to reach Leah's inbox.

Leah and I were indiscriminately born into two different worlds. Operating outside the bounds of our own experiences and their distinct interpretations is not only exceedingly difficult, it invites unintentional inauthenticity into a conversation, and we both deserved better. Gradually loosening my grip, I decide to be kinder to myself.

Thankfully, as our communications continue, formalities evaporate and our exchanges flow with greater ease and casual language. Explanation points emerge and smiley faces flourish. Despite the sensitivity of what unites us, we carry on like comfortably-acquainted friends. In fact, I not only like Leah, but I grow to care about her tremendously. How could I not? She has chosen us to parent her child. No greater gift could be bestowed upon us and my heart bursts with gratitude.

I'm under no illusion that this is easy for her, but I never get the impression that Leah writes about this pregnancy with a wounded spirit. She tells me that the baby is kicking "like a little soccer player," and she applauds Thomas's graciousness as he reliably appeases her many cravings. She asks if we've yet to embark on the thrill of "baby shopping," expressing the fun in making purchases for little girls.

As Leah's twentieth birthday approaches, we reach out to Lorayne and ask if we can send a gift. Now familiar with some of Leah's favorite treats, we propose a gift basket filled with these goodies. Lorayne thinks it's a great idea so we custom-tailor an order and have it sent to her. We're a little apprehensive about Leah's perception of this gift, but that's instantly squashed when she emails with a heading "You guys are so awesome" and writes that we made her birthday "even more special."

About a month after our initial contact, we begin to amass the essentials for parenthood. Leah asks what we've gotten and wants to hear about the color selection for the nursery. I tell her that we bought a car seat and stroller, but exclude that I painted the nursery in anticipation of the Moroccan babies. Instead, I describe the pattern of the crib's bedding and my plans to paint a mural on one wall. I let her know that Russ has been immersed in a thick, academic-like textbook gaining wisdom on raising a baby. She finds this hilariously endearing.

One day, Leah emails to tell me that the baby is breech and she's really pained with physical discomfort. With no deviation from her usual thoughtfulness, Leah considerately tells me that the baby is likely to turn on her own and not to worry. Though I'm relieved to hear this, I'm concerned for Leah's health. Planning to talk to her gynecologist about the pain, she mentions her doctor's abrasive manner and "rough" examinations. Reading that makes me cringe and bubble with anger. Aware of her adoption plans, Leah's doctor should be treating her with added compassion, not gruff severity. I want Leah showered in kindness with daily parades held in her honor. Ruminating how best to reply, I'm tempted to spew a mouthful of venom on this cruel physician. But instead, I fill the void with kindness. I venerate her strength, wish her an easier, less eventful nine weeks, and let her know that I will cheer for her until the pom-poms blister my hands.

We always inquire about each other's family, but our relationship is truly embedded in one another. Leah begins to initiate ending her emails with expressions of love, so it's not long before there's a natural exchange of "We love you guys!" And as if she grasps its significance, Leah always emails just before the start of a weekend. This not only bestows peace of mind that she remains intent on this adoption, but it also instills us with the confidence to advance preparations of welcoming a baby into our home.

Leah is the posterchild for ideal birth mothers, and with every email, my confidence in this adoption's success grows. She retains regular contact, never letting a week pass without an email. She doesn't express overly-sentimental feelings about the baby, but constantly demonstrates extreme care for her. One email includes the statement, "You guys are always in our thoughts… every time I choose a chicken sandwich over a cheeseburger." And filling my eyes with tears, she begins referring to the baby as "your baby."

It's now two months before the baby is due and I finally allow myself to purchase newborn clothes. This seemingly benign action has been tough to hurdle. I imagine innocuous questions from store clerks and passersby about the heap of newborn clothing in my shopping cart, curious since I'm visibly not pregnant. But the ghost of Morocco still lingers in the shadows and I'm just not ready to speak freely about this adoption. Although I'd like to see each article of clothing with my own eyes, and touch each piece with my own hands, I place an order online. Regardless, I relish every click and zoom, and by the time I'm finished, twenty-eight items fill my virtual cart.

The package arrives in a substantially-sized box and my belly surges with jitters upon its sight. I carry it inside and debate opening it. Although we've promised cautious optimism, I continually work to balance myself along the top of this narrow fence. One side protects with restraint while the other urges hope. I find my happy medium by removing each item from the box, handling every teeny garment with reverent and nervous fingers, but I leave their tags intact.

Several days later, Leah emails and tells me that the baby is no longer breech. I'm unsure of the details but knowing this alleviates pain for her, I'm thrilled by the news. However, for the first time in two months of emailing one another, she confides that seeing newborn outfits cause her to "tear up a little." These words, her brutal honesty... I *ache* for her. But she adds that they are "tears of joy to be a part of the soon-to-be joy of your lives." This incredibly perceptive young woman inserts subtle reassurances to communicate that she's still intent on proceeding with this adoption. It's as if she knows I could be twisted with anxiety over certain remarks if left open-ended.

Still, I worry that Leah masks her moments of sorrow with a brave facade. Perhaps this outward display sets the inward course. My sentiments are not derived of pity but overwhelming awe and admiration, because if roles were reversed, I don't know that I could remain as well-adjusted. I marvel at Leah's resolve and courage.

She ends the topic by telling me that her cure for these spells is to buy something new for her daughter. So she makes several small purchases.

**SHEER WILLPOWER**

# Emotional Vertigo

*"I'm not afraid of storms, for I'm learning how to sail my ship."* —Louisa May Alcott

During our commute into work this morning, at the drowsy pre-dawn hour of 5AM, Russ reminds me that a year ago today we were in Morocco. The comment bore no ill-intention and should have been regarded with the irony of comparison: where we were *then* to where we stand *now*. Leah is due in a mere six weeks and we are so very close to meeting a baby who will hopefully become our daughter. But finding it impossible not to glance in the rearview, my mind travels to the bleakness of our time in Morocco. Another agency, more emotionally-driven check-writing, another "maybe baby" dangled before us. Have we actually progressed or are we traveling a parallel route of doom? Before I can better stabilize my emotions, I stumble further when the radio commercial of our former fertility clinic airs, breezily promoting their many successes. I immediately change the station and Russ searches the darkness for my hand. And with his tight, reassuring squeeze of alliance, we continue our drive in bonded silence.

This adoption continues to proceed with textbook perfection and Leah's regular contact is a rare (and greatly appreciated) treasure. But as resolute as she feels today, she could change her mind tomorrow. Or, even more fearsome, she could reverse the adoption after the baby is in our care. These nagging risks hang over my head like a storm cloud deciding whether to unleash fury or abstain.

Although some days are dark, I mostly find myself residing in a state of perpetual limbo. I'm overjoyed that Leah and Thomas chose us and that a baby may very well join our family. But it is all veiled with a pointed, protective, and sometimes hardened layer of caution. This awareness has left me too overwhelmed to feel genuine, unhindered excitement. It's become very difficult to navigate these waters, deep with emotional vertigo. I just don't know which emotion is best to firmly affix myself. So like a merry-go-round, I revisit all with each passing revolution.

# The Birth of a Redefined Family

When establishing the framework for their adoptions, prospective parents are given the choice of an open or closed adoption. Best explained by *FindLaw*, "A closed adoption means that there is no contact whatsoever between the birthparents and the adoptive parents and child after the adoption takes place. In fact, there may be no contact before the adoption. But nowadays, the domestic trend is toward open adoptions, in which all the parties to an adoption meet and often remain in each other's lives."[*] Adoptive parents make their own determinations regarding the relationships they want to maintain with their future child's biological parents, and admittedly, when we first signed with LCA, we were concerned about blindly entering into an open adoption agreement. There's an underlying fear in this unknown and we were resistant to its invitation. But Lorayne had explained that very few adoptions were closed, and if we had opted to travel that path, we'd face an exponentially narrowed funnel of birth parent consideration. She patiently detailed her many clients' positive encounters with open adoptions, from the perspectives of both birth and adoptive parents. Acknowledging that the entire experience was a plate of wild risks, we abandoned caution and ask for another serving, in pursuit of an open adoption.

---

[*] http://family.findlaw.com/adoption/open-vs-closed-adoption.html

I not only relish this decision but have become so very grateful for *Leah's* willingness to engage in an open adoption with us. My fear of trusting a stranger quickly dissolves and transforms to loving attention for her emotional health. Leah is mature, astute, and very capable of arriving at a judicious conclusion, but I worry that one day this very young woman may be walloped by a sense of regret. And I wrestle with how that could heal. Leah has been pedestaled high within our hearts and imaging her distressed in the future troubles me. So to cushion a possible fall, I alter our pre-established parameters to limits set with the rigidity of a marshmallow wall. When first matched, Leah exclusively opted to receive emailed photos. I let her know that if she should change her mind and want to spend time with the baby, she'll have a warm bed awaiting her arrival. This child will not only understand that she was adopted, but she'll know the name of the woman who sheltered and cared for her so greatly in utero.

Surprising even us, this relationship has evolved beyond the baby. I convey to Leah that we will always welcome her in our lives, and that in its own unique way, we are a newly-sculpted version of family. What feels most important to communicate is our flexibility in direct conjunction with her happiness. She replies, "Thanks again for all the support... it has been the best experience ever," and words that resonate to the core of my soul, "I knew picking you and Russ was so right!"

A week later, Leah emails me about her steady health, a funny anecdote regarding her daughter, and a family gathering held that past weekend. At the email's end, she adds that they met with the adoption lawyer so Thomas could legally supply consent with his signature. Under the circumstances, this meeting could have been both somber and stressful but Leah mentions that the lawyer spent time chatting with them and playing with their daughter. I'm relieved that she references it with a light hand.

## SHEER WILLPOWER

Like a broken record, I consistently thank Leah for her emails, letting her know just how much we appreciate not only the health-related updates but our budding relationship. She replies, "I definitely love emailing you!" Leah tells me that the support I've offered has been "…much needed and appreciated." She adds, "I cannot wait to meet you guys and the baby!"

I feel like the stars are aligning.

Leah specifically asks if we selected a "take home outfit," for the baby, the clothing she'll wear when we leave the hospital. She says that her mom believes babies should be dressed in the color yellow for this momentous occasion, as it brings good luck. So we decide to honor that belief. I order a newborn outfit in soft yellow and pack it along with the other clothing, placing it closest to the pile's top.

My personal experience with pregnancy was short-lived, but while it lasted, I was consumed by a wealth of elated emotions. Aside from having none of the physical indicators, the sentiments that arise with adoption are an unexpected match. But there is one exception encapsulating a component that pregnancy omits. The depth of my love for Leah, under these peculiar set of circumstances, resides on an alternate plane of fundamental gratitude. After what feels like a lifetime of struggle, pain, and heartache, liberation arrives in the form of strangers declaring that *you* are their choice. Your anguish is healed with the gift of their child.

On the fourth of April, Leah emails, declaring that she's anxious to give birth. She wants to shop for a new bathing suit and take walks on the beach without the discomfort of pregnancy. Her due date is not for another two weeks but she feels like delivery is near.

We began our relationship a mere three months earlier and suddenly, it is forever changed. This was the last email I receive from Leah before she gives birth to a seven pound, two ounce baby girl.

**SHEER WILLPOWER**

LAURI M. VELOTTA-RANKIN

## Our Journey Ends (and Another Begins)

*"Not flesh of my flesh, nor bone of my bone, but still miraculously my own. Never forget for a single minute, you didn't grow under my heart but in it."*
—Fleur Conkling Heylinger

The clock hovers around 4AM and I'm summoned for a third time, awoken by the sharp, spastic cries of a hungry newborn demanding a bottle and fresh diaper. I strip the covers from my body to rise, and with zombie-like finesse, wearily shuffle my feet to the adjacent nursery.

Simone's mouth clumsily seeks the bottle's nipple and begins to pull at its contents. Her eyes close, forming two delicate slits as she nourishes. The pediatrician had suggested gently blowing on her face if she falls asleep while eating, and I've already employed this effective waking strategy several times. Her face twitches with surprise and her mouth promptly reengages. It's the sweetest thing I have ever witnessed.

Once she's completed her meal and is content with the escape of a small burp, I remain seated in the rocker awhile longer, allowing it to silently carry us with a gentle and hypnotic cadence. Simone's weight settles in my arms as she drifts to sleep. I can safely place her back in the crib without waking but I delay. Despite the multiple nighttime interruptions and sleep deprivation, something magical exists during these quiet moments together when the world slumbers around us. So I absorb it longer. My appreciation for this moment is soul-quenching, releasing an unmatched serenity.

I exhale deeply and reflect on the past several weeks. Our first few days as new parents were tumultuous. We were legally obligated to remain in New York with Simone until given consent from a myriad of adoption-related authorities. Catherine told us it could take up to ten business days, so we hunkered down in our hotel suite and prepared for the extended stay.

But complications arose the first night Simone was released from the hospital. Her crying was as perpetual as her breath. Sleep was scarce and despite following the hospital's feeding schedule (meticulously documenting date, time, and amount ingested), Simone was highly unsettled. Tiny beads of sweat formed on her nose and with strained cries, she struggled through a bowel movement. So we scheduled an appointment with the pediatrician who examined Simone at the hospital. She recommended gas drops and advised us to increase Simone's formula dosages, but it did little to alleviate the crying. With no improvement by 3AM the following morning, we called the emergency number the pediatrician had provided. Russ spoke with the on-call doctor. Instead of offering advice or direction, he lectured Russ about adopted children and detachment issues, as if her body was revolting over the fact that we weren't biologically related. When the call ended, we were both more stressed than prior to dialing the number. We spent the next two hours trying to soothe our newborn in the confines of a hotel room.

The tone of Simone's cry began to morph with the raised pitch of desperation. She grew hot with fever and by 5AM, we were in the emergency room. Her teeny, flailing body was placed on a hospital bed and she was instantly engulfed by a team of doctors and nurses. While the hospital pediatrician had suggested we increase Simone's formula dosage, the ER doctor admonished us for overfeeding her. He scathingly explained that her stomach was the size of her own fist and couldn't handle the amount we had allowed her to ingest.

Our heads spun with worry, confusion, and totaling ten hours of sleep over the past three nights, utter exhaustion. I was really beginning to feel like a failure, a woman unfit for motherhood. I presumed I would know how to care for my child. I thought it would blossom the moment Simone was placed in my arms, a dormant but ingrained trait. Yet here I stood, before a doctor who treated me with disdain, as if nonverbally communicating that I wasn't suited for this new role as a mother.

On the evening of our sixth day in New York, we received the call we had been so anxiously awaiting: we had legal permission to leave the state with our daughter and return home. We packed our bags, loaded the car, and commenced our drive home to Virginia late that night.

I sat beside Simone's car seat and held my breath every time she stirred. How would I soothe a newborn in these restraints? I was also worried about the volume of her cries in such a small space and the distraction that would cause for Russ while he drove. He, too, was gravely deprived of sleep.

But with the habits of most new parents, Russ drove with exceptional care. We stopped around 2AM to change Simone's diaper in a well-lit but empty McDonald's parking lot. We placed Simone on the heated passenger seat and standing just inside the door, I carefully cleaned her. Russ stood guard behind me, surveying the lot for danger. Simone

## SHEER WILLPOWER

cried with resistance throughout the changing, but once we were back on the road, she graciously opted to fall back asleep.

As we approached our home, the kindness of friends and neighbors was displayed in personified celebration. Illustrations made from sidewalk chalk decorated our driveway while banners with sweet messages were displayed by our front door. Balloons and pink tulle were tied to every post on our front porch and mailbox. My weary eyes welled with surprise by the touching gesture. Simone was being welcomed with love.

Our relief to be home was soon overshadowed by our priority to have Simone checked by a local pediatrician. Having already selected one, we called her office the minute it opened. I explained our adoption of a newborn and concerns over her eating and bowel movements. We were given an appointment that same morning.

Dr. Jamey performed a thorough examination. Her demeanor was kind, yet straightforward. As the stethoscope roamed Simone's chest, she spent an unusually long time silently listening. She gently lifted Simone out of my arms and cradled her as she shared a startling discovery. While we expected to hear about a change in formula or diagnosis of colic, she revealed that Simone likely has a significantly-sized hole in her heart. Dr. Jamey explained that the larger the hole, the more difficult detection becomes—which is likely why it was missed by the doctors who saw her in New York. It was mid-morning on a Friday and she didn't want us waiting until Monday to see a pediatric cardiologist. So she personally contacted one, scheduling us for the next morning.

And she also recommended a change in formula.

We left Dr. Jamey's office with brutally mauled emotions. Abject fear and burgeoning distress now accompanied utter exhaustion. While

Simone had survived countless fits of turbulent cries, I began to feel sheer panic when she exhibited the slightest degree of agitation.

We rose with the bleary eyes of new parents early that Saturday and embarked on a 40-minute drive to the cardiologist who was available for weekend appointments. The office was moderately busy, but we were seen immediately. Simone's torso was soon overrun with stickers for an electrocardiogram (EKG), her tiny chest offering minimal real estate for the numerous connections necessitating an accurate assessment. We were then ushered into a darkened room where Simone was laid prostrate while a technician ran the wand of an ultrasound over her chest. Studying the display of a monitor, she asked us to keep Simone still for the most accurate reading. We had little (if any) control over her movements, but luckily, Simone inadvertently obliged. We watched as our precious baby underwent a variety of daunting tests with machinery emitting a range of unexplained tones in cold, sterile rooms. I was overrun with stress and plagued by the unknown. Retaining my composure was a nearly impossible feat.

We had only been parents for one week.

The cardiologist revealed that there were two holes in Simone's tiny heart. We were directed to return for semi-regular check-ups but the doctor assured us that the holes' placements were not a serious concern.

Our new life started to better calibrate over the following few weeks. Simone's formula, changed four times, was now a better fit for her digestion. And an over-the-counter medication assisted with more manageable diaper habits.

It was a bumpy ride, but motherhood both fulfills and honors me. A little wear and a few washes allowed it to stretch at the seams and

## SHEER WILLPOWER

soften, perfecting its fit. I didn't *choose* to love Simone, I just did. The suggestion of choice is akin to stating that I have given permission for my heart to beat. I simply and purely have an innate connection to her soul that reprogrammed my entire world. My life is beautifully and forever altered.

This silent moment in a softly lit nursery with my daughter is profound and presents a new lucidity. It was as if I had lived thirty years never knowing the color yellow and suddenly found myself standing before a bursting sunrise. My journey has ultimately led me to a discovery of realignment. And I am finally in my right space.

LAURI M. VELOTTA-RANKIN

## In Reflection

*"The two most important days in your life are the day you are born and the day you find out why." –Mark Twain*

Most of my life was spent floating at the surface, unaware of the depth beneath. This experience yanked me under, choking, panicking, gasping for air. It challenged with ripples of personal trials and awoke me from a sleep of limitations. Without the entirety of this journey, I fear I'd still be asleep to the internal revolution that sets your soul aflame when tussling with life-defining struggle.

I've emerged in a baptism of gratitude, a discovery of widened perspective, and a recognition of the beauty captured within the moments of life's most difficult battles.

I have awakened.

Equally besieged, our frail maple tree was engaged in an arbitrary battle imposed by nature, but it responded with personified endurance. I mostly observed this tree from behind the glass of windows but identified it as a reflection, its prevailing strength my own. I cannibalized this symbolism, digesting it as energy for my own fight. I slipped into the skin of that tree, its bark a coat of armor, my

## SHEER WILLPOWER

feet embedded into its roots for stabilization. I too withstood the severity of my environment.

And in the end, my life was reflected in its sunlit leaves and my future visible in the buds emerging with triumphant vitality.

LAURI M. VELOTTA-RANKIN

# Advice for My Fellow Passengers

While many women admire the tan lines graced by sunny skies aboard this cruise ship, you and I hover over a toilet below deck, sick with nausea from this rocking vessel of hell.

Whatever the culprit, our biology does not permit a pregnancy to flourish the good old-fashioned way. That revelation can spiral you into an extensive tailspin. And it's not an easy stumble from which to rise. I empathize and can offer some "lessons learned," insight gathered from a series of poor decisions, blunders, and self-examination that led to several lucid revelations.

*Give yourself permission to grieve.*

Should you trek an unconventional path, bits of predefined womanhood will be lost. You'll never experience the anticipation of peeing on a stick and its magnificent reveal. Instead, you may become the friend turned to when another suffers a miscarriage because you've been through one (or two or many). You may find yourself involved in an exchange where a once-close friend uncomfortably divulges her pregnancy while backing towards the door, altogether vanishing from your life. Or conversely, have a friend so overcome with the wonderful news that conversations are overrun with its every detail, her somehow forgetting your circumstance. An added abrasion may arise when browsing headlines or scrolling through social media. Links to articles about breastfeeding and doulas, birth announcements, online photos of friends' children with comments reading the likes of "She's your mini-me!" And the painful reminder of what you battle to become while others celebrate it: Mother's Day. Occasionally, these instances glide by without notice or significant affect, and other times they devour your spirit. Borrowing the words of one of my literary idols, Elizabeth Gilbert answers this struggle: "The women whom I most admire in the world are those who have lived long and survived much. They have been through love, amazement, loss, catastrophe, sorrow. Most of all, though, they have been through DISAPPOINTMENT—and they have each individually found a way to live through it. Not only have they lived through disappointment; they came out on the other side much stronger as a result, having earned perspective, endurance, and wisdom through their trials."

*Be gentle with yourself.*

The process to grow your family may surprise with effortlessness, or it may strike with an onslaught of obstacles. If you're of the latter group, take a breather and escape the baby madness. Plan something indulgent and fantastically distracting for an hour, a day, a week. Return to it only when your swollen emotions and blood pressure have normalized. Don't hate your body for its struggles, and don't consume the failures outside your grasp. Your worth as a woman is neither defined by nor confined to the empty space inside your uterus. Make peace with yourself. And remember that your strength is present even when you doubt, or outright deny, its existence.

*Formulate a plan before you begin—and have multiple alternatives waiting in the wings.*

Those able to naturally conceive don't need a strategy beyond healthy eating, regular medical check-ups, and a bottle of cheap Chianti. But you, my friend, your preparation includes a suit of emotional body armor. Your emergency escape plan necessitates a precisely mapped route so when that fire alarm begins to siren, the thick smoke won't matter because you already know where and how to find your exit.

Assess and take inventory of finances, preferences, plans of action, and undeterred grit. Hope for the best, plan for the worst. Budget the cut-offs. Have the hard conversations with your partner and articulate those scary thoughts. Address the walls of restriction. Which option is ideal? What are you willing to do? How much money are you prepared to spend? And perhaps the toughest, where is your line drawn? What is your breaking point? This exchange is exceedingly crucial.

*Stick to your guns, but remain open to options.*

Establishing personal parameters is a commonsense stipulation for virtually every aspect of life. And while familiarity with the outermost edges of your comfort zone is essential, there are rare circumstances when these boundaries are adversely restrictive. Sometimes pushing it back a few inches illuminates new opportunities. I'm not suggesting bending principles, but rather recognizing the advantages of flexibility.

When deciding to pursue domestic adoption, we feared the shadowy "open adoption." A popular women's television channel practically produces a new movie about it annually: unstable birth mother terrorizes adoptive parents, frantic for child's return. Concerned about the contact with a birth mother, we preferred the safer, more distanced closed adoption. But the more we listened to the facts and permitted its consideration, we saw the unfair and inaccurate stigma. Ultimately deciding amenability to an open adoption greatly *eased* our worry, not elevate them. In addition to the updates on her health, Leah's emails served as confirmations that she planned to move forward with the adoption. And, those correspondences (which we've saved for Simone) are evidence of Leah's devotion to our daughter. We couldn't be more grateful for something we had originally shunned.

*Practice steadfast authenticity.*

Adoption forms come with a lot of blank boxes in pursuit of checkmarks, preceded by some very difficult questions. Before touching pen to paper, really scrutinize your selections. Take ample time for self-analysis and introspection. Be truthful to yourself and make peace with the uncomfortable stuff.

*Exercising kindness and employing instinctual acumen aren't mutually exclusive.*

Don't neglect to ask the tough questions out of fear. I was afraid of coming across as ungrateful or impolite so, much to my detriment, I frequently bit my tongue when dealing with both Lilith and Nada. Any legitimate adoption facilitator or medical professional understands, respects, and expects questions, even those that sometimes challenge. An impatiently curt, rushed, or poorly-addressed answer should give you pause. Although it often doesn't feel this way, you do maintain a degree of control in many of these family-growing options. Don't feel pressured and *always* trust your gut.

## LAURI M. VELOTTA-RANKIN

*Seize hold of your life-lines.*

As detailed earlier on, grief spiraled me into bleak withdrawal. In the wake of a mental earthquake, it's imperative to sort through feelings and restore internal order. Sometimes this is done with the help of close friends and/or family, while other moments favor housekeeping as a solo act. If you're a DIYer, just remember to eventually tap into a life-line and allow loved ones their support. Be forewarned though. As you approach dicey times, some friends mirror the behavior of sidewalk chalk: spectacular and vibrant in the sun, while washing away with the rain. Carefully weed through, and cherish those who remain by your side.

*Take pride in all personal triumphs, even those miniscule ones no one may notice but you.*

Earlier this year, I happened to catch one of the most coveted nominations for women during an awards show. Characteristically, a clip is played of the actress's performance in a movie followed by a live-shot of her sitting in the audience. And I noticed something peculiar, a reaction that made me rewind for a second look. I even tuned in longer than anticipated because I was curious to see if the men behaved similarly, which they didn't. What did I observe? All but one of the females demurely turned her head—to the right, left, down—as if embarrassed. But the attention was earned and well-deserved. They were the recipients of praise for their achievements. Why do so many of us squirm when our accomplishments are recognized?

We often don't permit ourselves rewarding or proud thoughts, especially those not dared to be publicly acknowledged. Rallying against that unjust mentality, I marvel when surveying the war zone remnants in my wake. And despite its trail of empty Kleenex boxes, I rather quickly overcame each impeding hurdle. I plowed forward

## SHEER WILLPOWER

despite many instances of being knocked to my knees. Weary with each setback, I may have been slower to rise and find my footing, but I always did. Hell, even crawling on hands and knees moves you forward. Sometimes surviving one lousy blood withdrawal at the fertility clinic was reason to celebrate. And with each progression, I surprised no one more than myself as I evolved into a resilient fighter.

*Don't necessarily expect closure.*

The concept of closure is a bit of an illusion to me because it signifies an ending—and I can't fathom an ending to this story because it's embedded in my soul. I have a symbiotic sense of pride and humility in the teachings of my experience. The components entrenched in grief and sadness helped direct me. But even now, several years past the hardship and finally mom to a daughter who has vividly beautified my world, I still feel the occasional jolt. There are times when my throat constricts while watching viral videos where loved ones learn of pregnancies. When filling out medical forms that require a disclosure of my miscarriage and ectopic pregnancy, I can't help but feel sorrowful. And sometimes my belly flops upon receiving photo holiday cards adorned with the smiles of sibling groups. I'll always think of those Moroccan children we didn't parent and those pregnancy losses. And although I'll never be comfortable with the term "closure," I have found peace despite it.

*Find your power.*

Standing tall or behaving with refined stoicism is not only needless, it's irrelevant. You can tremble and weep and find many occasions to doubt yourself. But your power is recovered in that single step forward. It's worth the repeat: just one, small advancement following a blow exponentially restores hope. While I don't hold the gold in courage, I happily accept the title of junior ambassador for the scrappy underdogs who brawled.

*Compassion is half the battle.*

Be kind to those who don't know how to speak to you about these struggles. It's difficult for friends and family to navigate the emotions of a fertility-challenged loved one. Their approach may be awkward as they painfully stumble over words. But realize that they're likely scrutinizing, meticulously selecting, and even rehearsing each carefully-composed comment and question about your well-being. Their remarks may, at times, seem inappropriate and our reactions can be unpredictable. A seemingly innocent remark may be received with inexplicable volatility or inconsolable tears. It's difficult to know what to say when we suffer a setback and the territory becomes even more perilous when they find themselves pregnant. There are no staunch guidelines, no fail-proof words, no consolation that is applicable to all. But if you can locate the good will and support hidden within their words, well that's half the battle.

*Embrace the pain and seek lessons hidden within.*

I sailed through many days without elevated sadness about our situation, but those unexpected disruptions would thrust me right back down the hole. The infant formula mistakenly delivered to our home, the fraudulent baby store purchases on my credit card, the morning commute's radio commercial for our fertility clinic, our local hospital's junk mail with "The Birthing Inn" written on the envelope. On most occasions, I could shake free of these. But sometimes they just stuck to my skin like leeches.

Though my losses never defined me, they certainly became intertwined with my identity. Reaching motherhood doesn't clear debris from the many roads we travel to reach it. Keanu Reeves is quoted as saying, "Grief changes shape, but it never ends." Connecting my life with Simone fills my heart, but it does not void or necessarily heal past losses. Like the surgical scars across my belly, they will always remain with me. But loss is rarely bestowed without a gift.

A kind of forced sorting through feelings helped me locate my center with frequent apocalyptic breakthroughs. These led to spiritual recovery and personal reshaping. With each awakening, I was reminded that I am in possession of a mighty resilience. It's a tenacity I had often overlooked. But those moments when it emerged, it impressed no one more than me.

I also shed a skin of ignorance through the entirety of this experience. I learned that the universe's purpose doesn't align itself with your expectations. Good does not systematically beget good with a world automatically bestowing justice upon the well-intentioned. There is an arbitrary nature to life.

Martha Beck wrote an exceptionally beautiful book called *Expecting Adam*, documenting the story of her son with Down syndrome. In it, she poignantly states, "He is the one who taught me to appreciate rainbows—not only in the sky but also in lawn sprinklers and dishsoap bubbles and patches of oil. He is the one who stops, and makes me stop, to smell the bushes." And though I blindly passed them a thousand times before, my long journey has enlightened me to the glorious rainbows visible in oil slicks. My lens has been forever altered.

LAURI M. VELOTTA-RANKIN

# From the Outside In

Perhaps there are questions you'd really like to ask adoptive parents but, concerned about offending, you refrain. Or maybe these are privately pondered queries you wouldn't dare articulate aloud. I've gathered a few from both sides of the aisle and filled those blanks with answers. These are merely personal opinions, but I'd venture a guess that many adoptive families would likely concur.

*Why choose adoption over IVF?*

The reverse could be asked as well, but IVF is often placed on a higher rung of this family-building ladder. Regardless, they share the same very simple answer: it's a personal, gut decision.

A single friend of mine desperately wanted children, so she planned to use a sperm bank. But she soon learned that she couldn't produce a viable egg. She decided to ask her half-sister if she would donate hers. Egg retrieval is a difficult, unpredictable, and costly procedure. But her sister agreed and it worked. The sperm was chosen and an embryo was created. She carried a healthy baby boy to full-term and is an ecstatic new parent. She and her son share minimal DNA, but she desperately desired to carry a baby. Although I wouldn't walk her path, it wasn't mine to travel. I'm wowed by her determination and ultimate success.

Our plan yo-yoed (from adoption to IVF and back to adoption) but adoption had always been in both our hearts and was an easy decision.

*What was the cost?*

An honestly vague answer: a lot. Adoption costs are comparable to that of a mid-range to high-end vehicle. And an agency's stated cost may not include estimates for airfare or hotel stays, which could require multiple visits (for domestic adoptions too, if the family wants to meet prior to birth) and long stays (also applicable to domestic adoptions, depending on the state's requirements). If you're inquiring about adoption costs because you are information-gathering for a potential adoption journey, utilize Google for these answers, email agencies, or ask on message boards.

*Why was your child "given up?"*

This question is marginally appropriate for very close friends and family, and wildly unacceptable for others. (And if unsure of where you fall, then you have your answer: do not inquire.) Often layered and complicated, birth parents deserve a voice in its answer. "Giving up" a child is likely the most agonizing, difficult, and selfless decision they have ever confronted. If adoptive parents care to divulge this information, please safeguard it with the utmost privacy because it's really no one's business outside of those directly affected.

*How should I reference an adopted child's biological mother?*

Adoptive families understand that obscure, esoteric terms exist in the world of adoption, so grappling to find appropriate titles can result in verbal stumbles. I've been asked about Simone's "real mom" by both close friends and strangers. It justifiably bristles the feathers of many adoptive parents, and depending on the approach, I too can molt when hearing those two words. But I realize people just don't know what to call the woman who birthed my child. So instead of taking a stab to find an inoffensive title, just ask. "What do you call your child's biological mother/father/sibling/family?" It will be greatly appreciated.

Since we had a pre-established relationship with Simone's birth mom (a common moniker), we just refer to her as Leah. Simone even talks about how she "grew in Leah's belly."

So when in doubt, simply ask—unless the person you're asking is a stranger. If that's the case, please recognize that it is an intrusion equivalent to an inquiry about the size of your underpants.

*Are you treated differently because you are an adoptive family?*

An adoption agency representative once told us that birth mothers tend to select women who resemble themselves. Simone's birth mother and I are both petite with olive skin and dark, curly hair. We could probably pass for cousins. I'm often told by relatives how much Simone resembles me as a child. Sometimes Simone asks if I can drape my hair over her head because it's an identical match in color and texture and she enjoys seeing herself with long, curly hair. Our physical similarities are ironic, though largely irrelevant. But due to this fact, most people are surprised to learn we're an adoptive family. So to strangers unaware of our adoptive family status, we're rarely given a second glance.

Dear friends of ours have an altogether different experience. Their adoptive family status is obvious to anyone with functioning eyes, and they have certainly been recipients of shocking remarks and disrespectful comments. What I've learned through their experience is the emotional damage caused by the ignorance of utter strangers. I am incredulous to discover just how often people feel compelled to inquire about the origins of their child.

Physical resemblance does not make a family. An adoptive child's parents are the people whose hands they hold when seeking comfort and security. They wake her with kisses in the morning, cuddle with her in bed at night, and take care of every need and want all the hours in between. They love no differently.

*Were you worried you wouldn't love your adopted child?*

I understand the question's intent, I really do. But I also think that as I'm unfamiliar with how it feels to love a biological child, those without adoptive children are at a loss to understand our love as well. And it's not just that love-upon-sight, but the gradual development of that love. We battled to reach parenthood, and entered that maternity ward with anxiety-riddled excitement and unabated fear. We were preparing to have a child given to us, literally placed into our arms, fully cognizant of the fact that her birth mother could reverse course. Simone could have legally been pulled from us days after we exited that hospital with her. That is, in a single word, *terrifying*. Perhaps our love was set in motion the moment we agreed to these terms and accepted the very unnerving potential consequences. I don't know who could agree to such conditions without a heart already bursting with love for an unborn child. So I speculate that when it comes to loving an unborn child, we followed a congruent path to biologically pregnant couples.

But a more direct answer would be no. No, I did not worry about developing love for Simone because that love existed before I even knew she did.

*Do you think you would love a biological child any differently (the implication being more)?*

Simone was not a consolation prize for the children who didn't manifest before her. And she certainly didn't replace the others. Disengaging from the contentious debate over life's inception, those two failed embryos were children we lost. Both sonogram photos are tucked away in a private, sacred place within our home. I've had occasions where good intentioned remarks abrade like painful rug burns: if our foreign adoption and pregnancies hadn't failed, our lives wouldn't have intersected with Simone's. I certainly understand the intent, but it's an awful comparison and universally erroneous.

If made to keep score, Simone has been my daughter for nine months less than mothers who birthed their children. That's all, nine months. If you're a mother to biological children, did you love your kids any less nine months ago than you do now? I didn't think so.

Simone is my every breath. She is my heart and she is my soul. She occupies space in the smallest atom of my body to its largest organ (the skin, interestingly enough). She is the sun to which my planet revolves. I could continue with the metaphors but I think I've exhausted the point.

My daughter is currently four years old and I can't bring myself to unplug the video monitor beside my bed. I peer into that tiny, blue-tinted screen, see the mass of black hair, and my heart swells with serenity. My little family often gathers around the computer to scroll through thousands (if not tens of thousands) of photos and videos from Simone's fifty-four months of life. And I can't (I simply *cannot*) endure these memories with dry eyes. "Happy tears" we tell Simone, which she now repeats when she catches a glimpse of my streaked face. I've just never felt anything like it. She pampers me with the purity of her love in the form of hugs and kisses, smiles and giggles. And she has no real comprehension of what she means to us.

Of course no one seeking children with their spouse wants to suffer biological roadblocks. I wanted to have a child with my husband and we were devastated when that failed. So would I have loved a biological child differently? Perhaps. "Differently" plays host to an ambiguously wide field of interpretations. But what I do know, with absolute certainty, is that I could not love a child any more than I love my daughter.

LAURI M. VELOTTA-RANKIN

## Dear Reader,

Your reviews are essential to the visibility and success of this book. Please take a moment to find *Sheer Willpower: A Mutiny to Motherhood* on Amazon and write a review. Thank you for your support.

*Lauri*

P.S.

Although my story has ended, this journey continues. Please join our community as we persist in this mutiny to motherhood—together.

SheerWillpower.com

twitter.com/SheWill_M2M

facebook.com/SheWill.M2M

youtube.com/channel/UCWvbykyRGvTS1QinuRFTfxQ

Made in the USA
Middletown, DE
07 August 2017